HOW TO READ THE
BIBLE
WITH UNDERSTANDING

How to Use Biblical Keys to Rightly Divide the Word of God and Enjoy the Bible

DEAN J. SANDELL

WESTBOW
P R E S S®
A DIVISION OF THOMAS NELSON
& ZONDERVAN

WestBow Press books may be ordered through booksellers or by contacting:

WestBow Press
A Division of Thomas Nelson & Zondervan
1663 Liberty Drive
Bloomington, IN 47403
www.westbowpress.com
1 (866) 928-1240

ISBN: 978-1-5127-8048-2 (sc)
ISBN: 978-1-5127-8049-9 (hc)
ISBN: 978-1-5127-8047-5 (e)

Library of Congress Control Number: 2017905047

Print information available on the last page.

WestBow Press rev. date: 4/5/2017

CONTENTS

PREFACE

MY JOURNEY IN studying the Bible began back in 1973. I had been three years out of high school with no direction in my life. I was in what I refer to as my "unformative" years. I had gotten to a point at one time that I considered suicide as my only alternative. I had a genuine love for God since my youth, but my knowledge and understanding of Him was limited. I thought that He was a vengeful God and was willing to zap me for any mistakes I made. I remember sitting on the steps of my parents' home in Birmingham, Alabama and I cried out to God, "you have to let me know who you are".

Some time later I met a person who invited me to take a class that taught you about the Bible. But it wasn't just about the Bible, but *how* to "rightly divide" it. This term, which we will be looking at in our study, is found in 2 Timothy 2:

> 15 Study to shew thyself approved unto God, a workman that needeth not to be ashamed, rightly dividing the word of truth.

I knew nothing about the Bible much less about "rightly dividing" it, but as I mentioned, I had an innate love for God and was interested in learning more. This person handed me a card that had ten benefits listed that I would learn from this class. I don't remember the ten, but the one that stood out to me was, "teaches you to discern truth from error". You see the Bible tells us in I Corinthians 12:

> 2 Ye know that ye were Gentiles, carried away unto these dumb idols, even as ye were led.

From the moment we are born we began to be "led". I get a kick out of seeing a mother carrying her infant baby around in a baby carrier. I look at the baby and think, "that baby has no choice but to go where mom is going", because the baby has no agenda of its own, but to be fed and have its diapers changed. I sometimes marvel at the beauty of the sight of a loving mother carrying for her baby.

But as we all know the baby grows up. It starts to make observations and as it gets older will make decisions based on their "being led". We live in an age of marvelous technologies because people were "led" to discover things that they used to advance mankind. Others are "led" to destroy mankind. Of course the usage of mankind is all inclusive and includes women.

This is the same regarding God. Depending on how we are "led", will determine our opinions about God. If we are "led" by truth, we will have a true knowledge and opinion about God. If we are "led" in error we will obviously have false knowledge and opinions about God.

The foundational verse in that class is found in John 10:

> 10 The thief cometh not, but for to steal, and to kill, and to destroy: I am come that they might have life, and that they might have it more abundantly.

I knew a little bit about Jesus, but I had no idea about a thief. I had heard that Jesus came to save us from our sins, which is true, but I had heard nothing about a more abundant life. We will be looking at this verse in our study.

So I took that class and it lived up to every claim it made. It changed my life. I had hope, I learned that God actually loved me, and yes, it taught me to "discern truth for error". And to this day, some forty plus years later I still use these principals in my study of the Bible and my daily life. Is my life idyllic and without problems? Of course not. Do I have victories over the thief? YES!!!!

One of the things I learned in the class was, "man's basic spiritual problem is the integrity and accuracy of the Word of God." These spiritual problems start with not reading the Bible. The next problem happens when the Bible is read but without an accurate understanding of it. The problem of not reading the Bible starts with, not knowing HOW to read it. The other problem stems from reading the Bible, but without accuracy.

It is my hope that after you read this book you will receive these benefits and more and that it will,

Show how the Bible interprets itself

Explain Bible contradictions

Show you that God is good ALWAYS

Teach you to pray effectively

Teach you to be victorious in life by defeating the enemy of God and man the Devil

Show you the importance of Jesus in our lives

Show you that God is light and that God is love

HOW to renew your mind so that you can demonstrate the power of God in your life

HOW to manifest the more abundant life that Jesus gave his life for

And of course, teach you to discern truth from error

My prayer for you in reading this book is the same that Paul prayed for the Ephesians.

Paul prayed Ephesians 1:

> 16 [I]Cease not to give thanks for you, making mention of you in my prayers;
>
> 17 That the God of our Lord Jesus Christ, the Father of glory, may give unto you the spirit of wisdom and revelation in the knowledge of him:
>
> 18 The eyes of your understanding being enlightened; that ye may know what is the hope of his calling, and what the riches of the glory of his inheritance in the saints,
>
> 19 And what is the exceeding greatness of his power to us-ward who believe, according to the working of his mighty power,
>
> 20 Which he wrought in Christ, when he raised him from the dead, and set him at his own right hand in the heavenly places,

21 Far above all principality, and power, and might, and dominion, and every name that is named, not only in this world, but also in that which is to come:

God wants us to know.

Before we begin our study I want to point out a few things. First, this is not a "new revelation". As I said, I took the class in 1973. I think it was new for that day and time. However, in the early 1900's a biblical scholar by the name of E.W. Bullinger wrote a book called, How to Enjoy the Bible, which is an exhaustive study of how the Bible interprets itself.

All this information, thanks to the day and time we live in with the internet, can be found. I simply have put together a collection of this information in a concise format so that it can be understood. It is what I would consider the foundation on how to rightly divide the Word whereas, Bullinger's work would be a much more in-depth study that the student can go to after having a basic foundation.

Throughout I will refer to the "Word of God" simply as "the Word". This is not to minimize the importance of God with His Word but for brevity and ease of reading I simply will refer to it as "the Word"

In English grammar the words Holy Spirit are generally always capitalized. You will see that at times I capitalize the words Holy Spirit and at other times I will spell them, holy spirit. This is not done hap-hazardly. When the words are capitalized I am referring to God who is THE Holy Spirit. When they are not capitalized I am referring to the holy spirit that God would put on people of the old testament and the holy spirit that we receive at the time of being born again, or the new birth. This is again not to minimize the importance of the gift of holy spirit but is to give clarity in understanding as to which is being talked about.

I suggest that if you are not familiar with reading the Bible and some of the passages that you read them slowly and let the words sink in a little. The Bible used in this study is the King James Version of 1611. It is the same Bible I grew up on and use today. It is written in Old English style with "thee's" and thow's and may at first be a little difficult to read but with time can be quite easy to read.

I am not saying by reading this book you will "understand" the Bible. That will take a lifetime of learning. There are parts that at times are not quite clear to me but as we continue to use the principals in this book, the Bible will open up to us as we grow. If when reading a portion of scripture seems unclear and you aren't able to get a grasp on it, leave trying to figure it out for another time and focus on scriptures that are clear. This will help in eliminating confusion. I do know from using these principles that knowledge and understanding of God is greatly enhanced.

There are things you will learn in this book that do not fit with traditional Christianity. It is not my intent to cause controversy. I am simply presenting the truths as I have learned them. Remember that it is always the integrity and accuracy of the Word of God that is always at stake. If tradition contradicts the truth then we must stand before God and let His Word stand.

Finally, I would like to thank, Westbow Press for all they did to produce this, my first, book. It was a wonderful experience to have such a top notch publisher handle the details involved in its production. Also, I have to admit that I took it upon myself to do my own proof reading and editing. I believe that I made all the necessary corrections to make reading this book enjoyable. However, if I should have missed something your understanding is appreciated.

Thank you for your time that you will be spending in this study. I know God will bless you richly.

Dean Sandell

INTRODUCTION

THE BIBLE IS by far the most misunderstood book in the world. Paradoxally, the Bible should be the most understood book in the world. I was taught years ago that the greatest secret in the world today is that the Bible is the revealed Word and Will of God. While some people may believe that, the Bible is still not understood when it is read. The simple reason for this is we were never taught *HOW* to read the Bible, which has lead to all the various religions that say they are based on the Bible.

Basic logic would dictate that a good and loving God would not make His will known in a multiplicity of ways and confusing manner. In fact God says in 1 Corinthians 14:

> 33 For God is not the author of confusion, but of peace, as in all churches of the saints.

The end result of not understanding the Bible when it is read, is that Christians are in a state of confusion and are defeated when God's will is just the opposite. Have you ever wondered what God's will is for your life? Is God a mean God? Is God a good God? We can only know by knowing His Word. But if we don't "rightly divide" it as God instructs us to, we will be defeated on every hand. If God instructs us to "rightly divide" His Word, as He does, then there must be keys and principals that will allow us to do it. 2 Timothy 2:

15 Study to shew thyself approved unto God, a workman that needeth not to be ashamed, rightly dividing the word of truth.

The importance of rightly dividing the Word is paramount. If it is, obviously wrongly divided, we will not have truth. God says in I Timothy 2:

4 Who will have all men to be saved, and to come unto the knowledge of the truth.

That truth can't be one truth for this person or that person of this or that group of people, it would have to be the same for everyone. Look at I Peter 1:

3 According as his divine power hath given unto us all things that pertain unto life and godliness, through the knowledge of him that hath called us to glory and virtue:

The only way we can have a "knowledge of him that hath called us to glory and virtue" is to study the Word of God, The Bible. Hebrews 4:

12 For the word of God is quick, and powerful, and sharper than any twoedged sword, piercing even to the dividing asunder of soul and spirit, and of the joints and marrow, and is a discerner of the thoughts and intents of the heart.

The Word of God is truly powerful, but only to the extent that we rightly divide it. Jesus made a comment to the Pharisees in Mark 7:

13 Making the word of God of none effect through your tradition, which ye have delivered: and many such like things do ye.

We can make the Word of God of "none effect" if we replace the truth of the Word with manmade doctrines and traditions. Instead of holding to what the Word says.

So why do we have the Bible in the first place? Jesus said it best in John 4:

> 24 God is a Spirit: and they that worship him must worship him in spirit and in truth.

That pretty much sums it up. God is spirit and we as humans can't see spirit with our five senses. In order for God to communicate with humans he has to come in some form that can be seen, such as the burning bush with Moses, or he can put His spirit upon or in someone and communicate that way. However, there is another way which He can communicate His will, and that is through His written Word which Jesus made known when He was on earth. He was the Word incarnate. He made known God's will by the way He lived his life. Jesus made a statement of himself in John 10:

> 10 The thief cometh not, but for to steal, and to kill, and to destroy: I am come that they might have life, and that they might have it more abundantly.

There are two entities mentioned here. There is the thief who comes, "not but for to steal, and to kill, and to destroy" and the other entity is Jesus who came "that they might have life, and that they might have it more abundantly." Mankind has an enemy and that is the devil or Satan whose sole purpose is to ruin people's lives. Job made a statement in Job 31:

> 35 Oh that one would hear me! behold, my desire is, that the Almighty would answer me, and that mine adversary had written a book.

God did eventually turn the captivity of Job and gave him double of what he had lost. BUT his adversary will never write a book. That's why understanding the Word is so important. There is a verse in I John 3:

> 8 He that committeth sin is of the devil; for the devil sinneth from the beginning. For this purpose the Son of God was manifested, that he might destroy the works of the devil.

Without knowing the Word, we will never be able to destroy the works of the devil. Notice that it also says, "for the devil sinneth from the beginning". The adversary works overtime to distort the truth about God and even himself to deceive people from knowing the truth about God and Jesus Christ. II Corinthians 4:

> 4 In whom the god of this world hath blinded the minds of them which believe not, lest the light of the glorious gospel of Christ, who is the image of God, should shine unto them.

One of his means to do this is found in II Corinthians 11:

> 3 But I fear, lest by any means, as the serpent beguiled Eve through his subtilty, so your minds should be corrupted from the simplicity that is in Christ.

And in verse 14 and 15 of II Corinthians 11 it says:

> 14 And no marvel; for Satan himself is transformed into an angel of light.

> 15 Therefore it is no great thing if his ministers also be transformed as the ministers of righteousness; whose end shall be according to their works.

The adversary will disguise himself as a minister of light to deceive mankind. We are warned in I Peter 5:

> 8 Be sober, be vigilant; because your adversary the devil, as a roaring lion, walketh about, seeking whom he may devour:

And in Ephesians 4:

> 14 That we henceforth be no more children, tossed to and fro, and carried about with every wind of doctrine, by the sleight of men, and cunning craftiness, whereby they lie in wait to deceive;

And in II Peter 2:

> 1 But there were false prophets also among the people, even as there shall be false teachers among you, who privily shall bring in damnable heresies, even denying the Lord that bought them, and bring upon themselves swift destruction.

God gave us His Word so that we can live victorious lives while here on earth and the adversary is working overtime to keep that Word, by whatever means, away from people so that they can't defeat him.

So just how did we get the Word and know that it can be trusted? Well the Bible gives us that answer as well. A verse found in II Peter 1:

> 19 We have also a more sure word of prophecy; whereunto ye do well that ye take heed, as unto a light that shineth in a dark place, until the day dawn, and the day star arise in your hearts:

> 20 Knowing this first, that no prophecy of the scripture is of any private interpretation 21 For the prophecy came not in old time by the will of man: but holy men of God spake as they were moved by the Holy Ghost.

This verse is very powerful. It tells us that the scriptures are not open to private interpretation. This raises the question. If it is of not of "any private interpretation", then how can it be interpreted? The only logical answer has to be, that it interprets itself. That is why we need to learn the keys to the Bibles interpretation so that we can rightly divide the Word. This verse not only tells us that the Bible is not any private interpretation, but gives the reason why. And that reason is, *For the prophecy came not in old time by the will of man: but holy men of God spake as they were moved by the Holy Ghost.* Do you remember earlier when I said that God could communicate with humans if He would put His Spirit upon or in a person? This verse explains that. Another verse gives us added insight on how we received the Word. II Timothy 3:

> 16 All scripture is given by inspiration of God, and is profitable for doctrine, for reproof, for correction, for instruction in righteousness: 17 That the man of God may be perfect, throughly furnished unto all good works.

This verse is also very informative. It tells us that, *"all scripture is given by inspiration of God"*. The words *"given by inspiration"* is the Greek word, *theopneustos* and means, "God breathed". It also tells us that it is, *profitable for doctrine, for reproof, for correction, for instruction in righteousness.* First it is "profitable", that means it will put us in the black so to speak. Businessmen know what it means to be in the black. Their making a profit. The scriptures are "profitable" for "doctrine" which is right believing. They are "profitable" for "reproof" which is to show us when we are not believing rightly. And they are "profitable" for "correction" which is to show us how to get back to doctrine or "right believing".

Finally, I want to look at one other verse in Galatians 1:

> 11 But I certify you, brethren, that the gospel which was preached of me is not after man. 12 For I neither received it of man, neither was I taught it, but by the revelation of (or from) Jesus Christ.

Paul made it clear that what he was teaching and writing to the church was not after man. He received the revelation of the Word from the spirit of Christ in him and he wrote what he was given. So if we put this together we will see that, *holy men of God spake as they were moved by the Holy Ghost,* that *all scripture is given by inspiration of God* which is God breathed, and that by *the revelation of (or from) Jesus Christ,* is how we received the Word of God.

As I close this introduction I want to look a very important verse in the Word. Revelation 22:

> 18 For I testify unto every man that heareth the words of the prophecy of this book, If any man shall add unto these things, God shall add unto him the plagues that are written in this book:

> 19 And if any man shall take away from the words of the book of this prophecy, God shall take away his part out of the book of life, and out of the holy city, and from the things which are written in this book.

God takes His Word very seriously because it is a matter of life and death to mankind. Just how seriously does God take His Word? Let's look as Psalm 138:

> 2 I will worship toward thy holy temple, and praise thy name for thy lovingkindness and for thy truth: for thou hast magnified thy word above all thy name.

God places His Word above His Name. If it is that important to God it should be that important to us. BUT is must be the "rightly divided" and, the accurate Word of God. God's Word's are life to those who believe them and death if not. The adversary is also very serious about God's Word because he knows that if he can keep the Word out of the hearts and minds of people he can control them and bring his will of stealing, killing and destroying to pass.

We will now begin to look at the keys and principals to rightly dividing the Word so that we can tap the promises that God has for us and defeat the adversary.

CHAPTER 1

Read What Is Written In The Verse

MAN'S BASIC SPIRITUAL problem is the integrity and the accuracy of the Word. People don't know how to read the Word or don't understand it when it is read. It therefore results in questions, confusion about God and ultimately unbelief.

The most basic place to start when reading the Bible is to simply read what is written in a verse. A large portion of the Bible will interpret itself right in the verse. Let's take a look at a few. Have you ever wondered what God's will for you is? The apostle John recorded in III John verse 2:

> 2 Beloved, I wish above all things that thou mayest prosper and be in health, even as thy soul prospereth.

Remember, John did the writing, but *what* he wrote was by inspiration or revelation from God. He wrote what God wanted written. Look what God is saying here and remember we simply have to read and add nothing to it. First we are called, "beloved". Next God says, "I wish above all things". That would indicate that this is foremost in God's mind and heart. Above all things means, "above all things". God has a reason for what He says in His Word, where He says it, when He says it, how He says it and to whom He says it. Here He is talking to His beloved and expresses a desire for them. What is that desire? *That thou mayest prosper and be in health.* Does that sound like an unloving God? Doesn't to me. There is a condition set forth for the fulfillment of this desire. *Even as thy soul prospereth.* The only means by which our souls can prosper is by studying the Bible, God's Word, and get it into our hearts and minds.

I want to look at the verses following verse 2. God goes on to say in verses 3&4:

> 3 For I rejoiced greatly, when the brethren came and testified of the truth that is in thee, even as thou walkest in the truth
> 4 I have no greater joy than to hear that my children walk in truth.

God says that He, rejoiced greatly. He also says that He has no greater joy than to hear that His children walk in truth. Imagine giving God joy! Nothing needs to be guessed at to understand these verses.

Another often quoted verse in the Bible is John 3:

> 16 For God so loved the world, that he gave his only begotten Son, that whosoever believeth in him should not perish, but have everlasting life.

Nothing too hard to understand in that verse. While that verse is often quoted the following verse gives us some insight. John 3:

> 17 For God sent not his Son into the world to condemn the world; but that the world through him might be saved.

Let's look at some more verses that can be understood just by reading the verse. I John 1:

15 This then is the message which we have heard of him, and declare unto you, that God is light, and in him is no darkness at all.

Since this verse states that, *"God is light, and in him is no darkness at all."*, then why are terrible acts attributed to God? Insurance companies actually have clauses that cover, "acts of God". Since God says that He is light and that there is no darkness at all in Him, it stands to reason that somebody has got to be a liar.

The Psalms are filled with, in the verse interpretations. Let's look at just a few. Psalms 1:

1 Blessed is the man that walketh not in the counsel of the ungodly, nor standeth in the way of sinners, nor sitteth in the seat of the scornful. 2 But his delight is in the law of the LORD; and in his law doth he meditate day and night. 3 And he shall be like a tree planted by the rivers of water, that bringeth forth his fruit in his season; his leaf also shall not wither; and whatsoever he doeth shall prosper.

Psalm 4:

4 Stand in awe, and sin not: commune with your own heart upon your bed, and be still. Selah. (Selah means pause and consider what has been said.) 5 Offer the sacrifices of righteousness, and put your trust in the LORD. 6 There be many that say, Who will shew us any good? LORD, lift thou up the light of thy countenance upon us. 7 Thou hast put gladness in my heart, more than in the time that their corn and their wine increased. 8 I will both lay me down in peace, and sleep: for thou, LORD, only makest me dwell in safety.

Psalm 5:

> 12 For thou, LORD, wilt bless the righteous; with favour wilt thou compass him as with a shield.

And of course a Psalm very familiar to many people is the 23rd Psalm.

> 1 The LORD is my shepherd; I shall not want.

> 2 He maketh me to lie down in green pastures: he leadeth me beside the still waters. 3 He restoreth my soul: he leadeth me in the paths of righteousness for his name's sake. 4 Yea, though I walk through the valley of the shadow of death, I will fear no evil: for thou art with me; thy rod and thy staff they comfort me. 5 Thou preparest a table before me in the presence of mine enemies: thou anointest my head with oil; my cup runneth over. 6 Surely goodness and mercy shall follow me all the days of my life: and I will dwell in the house of the LORD for ever.

That Psalm is only six verses long but is extremely powerful with the message it gives us about God. And all we have to do is read it and not add or subtract from it. So, as I mentioned a great part of the Bible can be interpreted and understood just by reading what's in a verse. We can now look at another principle in helping us to rightly divide the Word of Truth.

CHAPTER 2

Read What's Written In The Context

DID YOU KNOW that it says in the Bible that there is no God? It says it in Psalms 14:1. It is actually written there. But let's look at what Psalms 14 says

> 1 The fool hath said in his heart, There is no God. They are corrupt, they have done abominable works, there is none that doeth good

You can prove almost anything from the Bible if you wrongly divide it. As you can see from the context that is says, "the *fool* hath said in his heart".

Another example of the importance of attending to context appears in Romans 3:

> 23 For all have sinned, and come short of the glory of God;

This verse has been used by the adversary to beat Christians up and make them feel unworthy before God. But what does it say in the context? Romans 23:

> 20 Therefore by the deeds of the law there shall no flesh be justified in his sight: for by the law is the knowledge of sin.

21 But now the righteousness of God without the law is manifested, being witnessed by the law and the prophets; 22 Even the righteousness of God which is by faith of Jesus Christ unto all and upon all them that believe: for there is no difference: 23 For all have sinned, and come short of the glory of God; 24 Being justified freely by his grace through the redemption that is in Christ Jesus: 25 Whom God hath set forth to be a propitiation through faith in his blood, to declare his righteousness for the remission of sins that are past, through the forbearance of God;

In the context we can see that it is talking about the law and sin. But it is also talking about the righteousness of God which we receive by faith in Jesus Christ. Right after the verse in question it states, "being justified freely by his grace through the redemption that is in Christ Jesus". I can see why the adversary wouldn't want people to know their true standing in Christ, that God freely gives because then the believer can defeat the devil.

There is another verse used out of context that is found in the same chapter of Romans 3:

10 As it is written, There is none righteous, no, not one:

This verse also is used the beat up the Christian. But as we have seen the context of the chapter is the freely given redemption that is by faith in Jesus Christ.

Missionary's often use Psalm 2:8 when referring to saving souls for the lord Jesus Christ:

8 Ask of me, and I shall give thee the heathen for thine
inheritance, and the uttermost parts of the earth for thy
possession.

But what does the following verse say?

9 Thou shalt break them with a rod of iron; thou shalt dash
them in pieces like a potter's vessel.

That doesn't sound like a very loving way to treat someone you want
to win to Christ.

Let's take a look at a parable Jesus presented and see how the Word
interprets itself in the context. Mathew 13:

24 Another parable put he forth unto them, saying, The kingdom
of heaven is likened unto a man which sowed good seed in
his field:

Do we know from this verse what the good seed is? Not at this point.
Do we know what the field is? No

25 But while men slept, his enemy came and sowed tares among
the wheat, and went his way. 26 But when the blade was
sprung up, and brought forth fruit, then appeared the tares
also. 27 So the servants of the householder came and said
unto him, Sir, didst not thou sow good seed in thy field?
from whence then hath it tares? 28 He said unto them, An
enemy hath done this. The servants said unto him, Wilt thou
then that we go and gather them up? 29 But he said, Nay;
lest while ye gather up the tares, ye root up also the wheat
with them. 30 Let both grow together until the harvest: and
in the time of harvest I will say to the reapers, Gather ye

together first the tares, and bind them in bundles to burn them: but gather the wheat into my barn.From this reading, do we know who the enemy is, do we know what the tares are? Again, not at this point. Now if we wanted to we could guess at what they are but we don't need to guess. Jesus starts another parable in verse 31:

> 31 Another parable put he forth unto them, saying, The kingdom of heaven is like to a grain of mustard seed, which a man took, and sowed in his field: 32 Which indeed is the least of all seeds: but when it is grown, it is the greatest among herbs, and becometh a tree, so that the birds of the air come and lodge in the branches thereof. 34 All these things spake Jesus unto the multitude in parables; and without a parable spake he not unto them:35 That it might be fulfilled which was spoken by the prophet, saying, I will open my mouth in parables; I will utter things which have been kept secret from the foundation of the world.

After this Jesus stopped teaching. Verse 36 gives us some information about the disciples.

> 36 Then Jesus sent the multitude away, and went into the house: and his disciples came unto him, saying, Declare unto us the parable of the tares of the field.

Now those are some smart disciples. Instead of guessing between themselves what Jesus meant, they had the good sense to simply ask Jesus, "Declare unto us the parable of the tares of the field," Jesus then goes on to explain the parables.

> 37 He answered and said unto them, He that soweth the good seed is the Son of man;38 The field is the world; the good

seed are the children of the kingdom; but the tares are the children of the wicked one;39 The enemy that sowed them is the devil; the harvest is the end of the world; and the reapers are the angels.40 As therefore the tares are gathered and burned in the fire; so shall it be in the end of this world.41 The Son of man shall send forth his angels, and they shall gather out of his kingdom all things that offend, and them which do iniquity;42 And shall cast them into a furnace of fire: there shall be wailing and gnashing of teeth.

We now know that the sower, is the Son of man. We know that the field is the world, the good seed are the children of the kingdom, the tares are the children of the wicked one; the enemy that sowed them is the devil,the harvest is the end of the world; and the reapers are the angels.

We don't have to guess at what the Word is telling us. By using the simple key of reading what's written "in the context", we can let the Word interpret itself so that there is no confusion understanding the Word. We can now look at the next principal, "where it has been used before".

CHAPTER 3

Where It Has Been Used Before

I F WE CAN'T see the meaning from, "in the verse" or from the "context" we then can use the principal of "where it has been used before". One of the most misunderstood and guessed at passages in the Bible regards Paul's thorn in the flesh found in II Corinthians 12:

> 7 And lest I should be exalted above measure through the abundance of the revelations, there was given to me a thorn in the flesh, the messenger of Satan to buffet me, lest I should be exalted above measure.

There has been no end of speculation as to what was Paul's thorn in the flesh. From it being his eyesight to an illness to sexual desire, people have "guessed" at just what this thorn in the flesh was.

The context of this situation is found in II Corinthians 12:

> 3 And I knew such a man, (whether in the body, or out of the body, I cannot tell: God knoweth;)4 How that he was caught up into paradise, and heard unspeakable words, which it is not lawful for a man to utter.

Paul had received revelation regarding the third heaven and earth. This no doubt would have been a overwhelming and encouraging time for him. But as we read we are told that "there was given to me a thorn in the flesh, the messenger of Satan to buffet me, lest I should be exalted above measure."

We can learn from this that the messenger was from Satan and the purpose was to buffet him, but we don't know what the thorn in the flesh was because it doesn't tell us that here. However, by looking at previous usages of the term "thorn" we will be able to find out what the thorn was.

Let's look at Numbers 33. God is giving Moses instructions on what the children of Israel were to do after they inherited the promise land. In verse 51 we see the instruction from God.

> 51 Speak unto the children of Israel, and say unto them, When ye are passed over Jordan into the land of Canaan52 Then ye shall drive out all the inhabitants of the land from before you, and destroy all their pictures, and destroy all their molten images, and quite pluck down all their high places:53 And ye shall dispossess the inhabitants of the land, and dwell therein: for I have given you the land to possess it.

God then goes on in verse 55:

> 55 But if ye will not drive out the inhabitants of the land from before you; then it shall come to pass, that those which ye let remain of them shall be pricks in your eyes, and thorns in your sides, and shall vex you in the land wherein ye dwell.

It is apparent from this verse that a thorn in your side is people. Will they be putting literal pricks in their eyes or thorns in their sides? No, but by a figure of speech God is saying these people who you let remain will be very troublesome to you.

Let's look at another verse. Joshua 23:

> 13 Know for a certainty that the LORD your God will no more
> drive out any of these nations from before you; but they shall
> be snares and traps unto you, and scourges in your sides, and
> thorns in your eyes, until ye perish from off this good land
> which the LORD your God hath given you.

What are nations made up of? People!!!!!!!

One more verse. Judges 2

> 2 And ye shall make no league with the inhabitants of this land;
> ye shall throw down their altars: but ye have not obeyed my
> voice: why have ye done this?3 Wherefore I also said, I will
> not drive them out from before you; but they shall be as
> thorns in your sides, and their gods shall be a snare unto you.

God is very clear as to what the unbelievers would do to the Israelites
if they didn't get rid of them. Look at what people did to the apostle
Paul. II Corinthians 11:

> 24 Of the Jews five times received I forty stripes save one.25
> Thrice was I beaten with rods, once was I stoned, thrice
> I suffered shipwreck, a night and a day I have been in the
> deep;26 In journeyings often, in perils of waters, in perils of
> robbers, in perils by mine own countrymen, in perils by the
> heathen, in perils in the city, in perils in the wilderness, in
> perils in the sea, in perils among false brethren;

It is clear from out study of "previous usage" that Paul's thorn in
the flesh were people. These people were influenced by Satan and
worked to hinder Paul's ministry. We no longer have to guess what
Paul's thorn in the flesh was because the Word makes it clear for us

CHAPTER 4

To Whom It Is Written

THE ENTIRE BIBLE is not written to everyone. And without the understanding of to whom it is written can cause no end of confusion. We will see that God makes it clear as to whom He is addressing in different sections of the Bible. While we may be able to learn from a portion of scripture not written to us, to try to apply it when it doesn't apply to us could cause problems.

So let's start and look at some scriptures that tell us to whom they are written. Romans 1:

> 1 Paul, a servant of Jesus Christ, called to be an apostle, separated unto the gospel of God,2 (Which he had promised afore by his prophets in the holy scriptures,)3 Concerning his Son Jesus Christ our Lord, which was made of the seed of David according to the flesh;4 And declared to be the Son of God with power, according to the spirit of holiness, by the resurrection from the dead:5 By whom we have received grace and apostleship, for obedience to the faith among all nations, for his name:6 <u>Among whom are ye also the called of Jesus Christ:</u>7 <u>To all that be in Rome, beloved of God, called to be saints:</u> Grace to you and peace from God our Father, and the Lord Jesus Christ.

We can see from verses 6 and 7 that this is addressed to the Christian church at Rome. Let's look at 1 Corinthians 1:

> 1 Paul, called to be an apostle of Jesus Christ through the will of God, and Sosthenes our brother,2 <u>Unto the church of God which is at Corinth, to them that are sanctified in Christ Jesus, called to be saints,</u> with all that in every place call upon the name of Jesus Christ our Lord, both theirs and ours:

It is again clear to whom it is written, "unto the church of God which is at Corinth, to them that are sanctified in Christ Jesus, called to be saints". II Corinthians 1:

> 1 Paul, an apostle of Jesus Christ by the will of God, and Timothy our brother, <u>unto the church of God which is at Corinth, with all the saints which are in all Achaia:</u>

Here it is to, the church of God which is at Corinth. Again, Christians.

Let's look at the other epistles.

Galatians 1

> 1 Paul, an apostle, (not of men, neither by man, but by Jesus Christ, and God the Father, who raised him from the dead;)2 And all the brethren which are with me, <u>unto the churches of Galatia:</u>

Ephesians 1:1 Paul, an apostle of Jesus Christ by the will of God, <u>to the saints which are at Ephesus, and to the faithful in Christ Jesus:</u>

Philippians 1:1 Paul and Timotheus, the servants of Jesus Christ, <u>to all the saints in</u> <u>Christ Jesus which are at Philippi,</u> with the bishops and deacons:

Colossians 1:1 Paul, an apostle of Jesus Christ by the will of God, and Timotheus our brother, 2 <u>To the saints and faithful brethren in</u> <u>Christ which are at Colosse:</u> Grace be unto you, and peace, from God our Father and the Lord Jesus Christ.

This pattern follows through Thessalonians. The epistles of Timothy and Titus are addressed the particular people regarding matters of the Church.

In Romans 15 we find an enlightening scripture.

> 4 For whatsoever things were written aforetime were written for our learning, that we through patience and comfort of the scriptures might have hope.

The church as we know it was started on the day of Pentecost when there was an out pouring of the Holy Spirit. The "aforetime" is referring to the time before the day of Pentecost because, on that day things changed. We are told that "whatsoever things were written aforetime were written for our learning". Obviously we can learn a lot from the Old Testament. However, if we were to try to apply it in this day and time we would be snubbing what Christ did for us on the cross and through his resurrection.

God also states in I Corinthians 10 a similar statement.

> 11 Now all these things happened unto them [Isreal] for ensamples [examples]: and they are written for our admonition, upon whom the ends of the world are come.

God also refers to three classes of people in I Corinthians 10:

> 32 Give none offence, neither to the Jews, nor to the Gentiles, nor to the church of God:

So portions of the Bible are written to either the Jews or to Gentiles or the church of God. In the book of Romans is a good example of scripture being addressed to different groups of people. Romans 1:

> 7 To all that be in Rome, <u>beloved of God, called to be saints</u>: Grace to you and peace from God our Father, and the Lord Jesus Christ. Then in chapter 9 of Romans the subject changes, Romans 9:

> 1 I say the truth in Christ, I lie not, my conscience also bearing me witness in the Holy Ghost,2 That I have great heaviness and continual sorrow in my heart.3 For I could wish that myself were accursed from Christ for my brethren, my kinsmen according to the flesh:4 <u>Who are Israelites</u>; to whom pertaineth the adoption, and the glory, and the covenants, and the giving of the law, and the service of God, and the promises;

The object of his writing now has changed to the Israelites. Then in chapter 10 to whom Paul is writing is repeated. Romans 10:

> 1 Brethren, my heart's desire and prayer to God <u>for Israel</u> is, that they might be saved.

It's in this chapter that we find out about how to be saved. Romans 10:

> 8 But what saith it? The word is nigh thee, even in thy mouth, and in thy heart: that is, the word of faith, which we preach;9

That if thou shalt confess with thy mouth the Lord Jesus, and shalt believe in thine heart that God hath raised him from the dead, thou shalt be saved.10 For with the heart man believeth unto righteousness; and with the mouth confession is made unto salvation.

In Romans 10:1 Paul writes, "my heart's desire and prayer to God <u>for Israel</u> is, that they might be saved." He then goes on in verses 8-10 and tells them exactly how they, or anyone for that matter, may be saved. Paul goes on and in Romans 11 the subject changes again:

13 For <u>I speak to you Gentiles</u>, inasmuch as I am the apostle of the Gentiles, I magnify mine office:

In this one book God, through Paul, writes to the three categories of people. Starting with the Church, then the Jews and the Gentiles. In Romans 12 the object of his writing changes again. Romans 12:

1 I beseech you therefore, <u>brethren</u>, by the mercies of God, that ye present your bodies a living sacrifice, holy, acceptable unto God, which is your reasonable service.

2 And be not conformed to this world: but be ye transformed by the renewing of your mind, that ye may prove what is that good, and acceptable, and perfect, will of God.

Paul has now gone back to writing to the "brethren", those who have fulfilled Romans 10: 9&10. He instructs them in the first two verses of Romans 12, a very important principal that will cause them to walk in what Christ had accomplished, "the renewed mind". It is the renewing of our minds to God's Word that will prove "what is that good, and acceptable, and perfect, will of God." That's why it is so important to read and rightly divide the Word. If it is wrongly divided, we will not know the good, and acceptable, and perfect, will of God.

So where do the Gospels fit in this. To whom were they written? Let's look at Romans 15:

> 8 Now I say that Jesus Christ was a minister of the circumcision [Israel] for the truth of God, to confirm the promises made unto the fathers:

Romans 10:4 For Christ is the end of the law for righteousness to every one that believeth.

Jesus' ministry was to Israel and he was the end of the Law, because he fulfilled the law perfectly. Can we learn anything from the Gospels? I think the answer is obvious. There is no end to what we can learn from Jesus' teaching. But to put ourselves under the law would nullify his work on the cross and his resurrection. Let's look at a scripture that is written to us. Galatians 6:

> 15 For in Christ Jesus neither circumcision availeth any thing, nor uncircumcision, but a new creature.

Philippians 3:

> 3 For we are the circumcision, which worship God in the spirit, and rejoice in Christ Jesus, and have no confidence in the flesh.

So we can see the importance the principal of "to whom it is written". We so far we have learned to rightly divide the Word by, "read what's written in the verse", "read what's written in the context", "where it has been used before" and "to whom it is written". Next we will look at rightly dividing the Word regarding "administrations".

CHAPTER 5

Dispensations: (Administrations)

The book of Hebrews starts by giving us important information Hebrews 1:

> 1 God, who at sundry times and in divers manners spake in time past unto the fathers by the prophets,2 Hath in these last days spoken unto us by his Son, whom he hath appointed heir of all things, by whom also he made the worlds;3 Who being the brightness of his glory, and the express image of his person, and upholding all things by the word of his power, when he had by himself purged our sins, sat down on the right hand of the Majesty on high;

THE WORD SUNDRY means, "various, varied, assorted" and the word divers means, "many, numerous, multiple". God over the span of time, "spake in time past unto the fathers, by the prophets." Throughout time and history God was making Himself know in varied and multiple ways and He did this through His prophets. But, now in our day and time He speaks to us "by His Son". God has always wanted to make His will known to mankind. However, He had to adapt Himself to the condition of man at different times. He dealt with Adam and Eve one way before the fall and another way, after the fall. He dealt with Israel one way before the law and another way, after the law was given. This is true of future events that will come. Right now He speaks to us by His Son. After the return of Christ, He will deal with mankind differently.

You can think of the "dispensations" like that of a presidential "administration". When one president leaves office his "administration" is now over. The new president takes over and begins his "administration" or his way of doing things. This is the same with the "dispensations" in the Bible. As we look into this we will find that there are seven different "dispensations" that we can trace through the Word. I will refer to these as "administrations" because the Greek word for "dispensation" is, *"oikonomia"* and refers to the "act of administering". It is used in the Gospels as stewardship.

Paradise

The first administration was the *Paradise*. This started when God placed Adam and Eve in the garden. Genesis 1:

> 28 And God blessed them, and God said unto them, Be fruitful, and multiply, and replenish the earth, and subdue it: and have dominion over the fish of the sea, and over the fowl of the air, and over every living thing that moveth upon the earth.

It is apparent here that God had given Adam and Eve great authority over the earth. Genesis 2:

> 15 And the LORD God took the man, and put him into the garden of Eden to dress it and to keep it.

Adam and Eve were put in the garden to be productive and commune with God in fellowship. I would imagine that they had a pretty good thing going on. However, as we all know Adam and Eve sinned and turned the authority that God had given them over to the adversary and things changed. Genesis 3:

> 22 And the LORD God said, Behold, the man is become as one of us, to know good and evil: and now, lest he put forth his hand, and take also of the tree of life, and eat, and live for ever:23 Therefore the LORD God sent him forth from the garden of Eden, to till the ground from whence he was taken.24 So he drove out the man; and he placed at the east of the garden of Eden Cherubims, and a flaming sword which turned every way, to keep the way of the tree of life.

Patriarchal

Because of the change in circumstances, God had to now start dealing with mankind differently. The next administration is known as the *Patriarchal* . This is the time before the Law was given to Moses and had the patriarchs like Noah, Abraham, and Isaac. It is interesting to note that mankind had a way back to God through "sacrifice" because we are told in Genesis Genesis 4:

> 1 And Adam knew Eve his wife; and she conceived, and bare Cain, and said, I have gotten a man from the LORD.2 And she again bare his brother Abel. And Abel was a keeper of sheep, but Cain was a tiller of the ground.3 And in process of time it came to pass, that Cain brought of the fruit of the ground an offering unto the LORD.4 And Abel, he also brought of the firstlings of his flock and of the fat thereof. And the LORD had respect unto Abel and to his offering:5 But unto Cain and to his offering he had not respect. And Cain was very wroth, and his countenance fell.

We also know from 2 Peter 2:

> 5 And spared not the old world, but saved Noah the eighth person, a preacher of righteousness, bringing in the flood upon the world of the ungodly;

So, a knowledge of God was available, but mankind didn't receive it. Romans 12:

> 12 For as many as have sinned without law shall also perish without law: and as many as have sinned in the law shall be judged by the law;

And we see also a reference to this administration in Acts 17:

> 30 And the times of this ignorance God winked at; but now commandeth all men everywhere to repent:

Law

The next administration was the Law Administration. We find in Malachi 4 a reference to this.

> 4 Remember ye the law of Moses my servant, which I commanded unto him in Horeb for all Israel, with the statutes and judgments.

We see here that God gave Moses the Law for all Israel, with the statutes and judgments.

Before the Law was given there was no transgression, because there were no statues and judgments to go by. But after the Law, a standard was available to go by and not doing it became sin. Romans 10:

> 5 For Moses describeth the righteousness which is of the law,
> That the man which doeth those things shall live by them.

There was a righteousness, but you had to live according to the Law to receive it. This required quite a bit of work on peoples part to obtain it. If it had been possible to obtain the righteousness that God had intended it would have been in the Law. Galatians 3:

> 5 For Moses describeth the righteousness which is of the law,
> That the man which doeth those things shall live by them.

Scripture in Galatians and Romans gives us insight regarding the Law. Galatians 3:

> 24 Wherefore the law was our schoolmaster to bring us unto [until] Christ, that we might be justified by faith.

And Romans 10:

> 4 For Christ is the end of the law for righteousness to everyone that believeth.

Christ

Well, God had a plan that He set forth in Genesis after the fall. The next administration was the *Christ* administration.

Christ came to Israel. Israel lived under the Law administration. Upon the coming of Jesus the administration changed because of the physical presence of Jesus. Jesus came to fulfill the Law which no other person could do. Jesus miraculous conception by the Holy Spirit was the start of God's plan to redeem mankind as God had promised in Genesis after the fall. Genesis 3:

15 And I will put enmity between thee and the woman, and between thy seed and her seed; it shall bruise thy head, and thou shalt bruise his heel

The announcement to Mary by the Angle Gabriel is very revealing about Jesus' purpose as recorded in the Gospel of Luke 1:

26 And in the sixth month the angel Gabriel was sent from God unto a city of Galilee, named Nazareth,

27 To a virgin espoused to a man whose name was Joseph, of the house of David; and the virgin's name was Mary.

28 And the angel came in unto her, and said, Hail, thou that art highly favoured, the Lord is with thee: blessed art thou among women.

29 And when she saw him, she was troubled at his saying, and cast in her mind what manner of salutation this should be.

30 And the angel said unto her, Fear not, Mary: for thou hast found favour with God.

31 And, behold, thou shalt conceive in thy womb, and bring forth a son, and shalt call his name JESUS.

32 He shall be great, and shall be called the Son of the Highest: and the Lord God shall give unto him the throne of his father David:

33 And he shall reign over the house of Jacob for ever; and of his kingdom there shall be no end.

34 Then said Mary unto the angel, How shall this be, seeing I know not a man?

35 And the angel answered and said unto her, The Holy Ghost shall come upon thee, and the power of the Highest shall overshadow thee: therefore also that holy thing which shall be born of thee shall be called the Son of God.

36 And, behold, thy cousin Elisabeth, she hath also conceived a son in her old age: and this is the sixth month with her, who was called barren.

37 For with God nothing shall be impossible.

38 And Mary said, Behold the handmaid of the Lord; be it unto me according to thy word. And the angel departed from her.

Those things listed in verses 32 and 33 were part of the promise God made to Israel. God could have provided the redeemer at anytime, for every woman starting with Eve was capable of bearing God's only begotten son, but He had to wait for a woman who would believe in order for Him to provide the seed necessary to bring about the conception of His son. He needed an Israelite woman who was looking for the redeemer as promised in the Old Testament who would believe. Look again at Mary's response to Gabriel's announcement in verse 38,

38 And Mary said, Behold the handmaid of the Lord; be it unto me according to thy word. And the angel departed from her.

She literally believed what the angel said to her and at that moment conception was made. It is interesting to note that while Israel was told in the scriptures that a redeemer was promised, Mary, who all her life was taught in the synagogues about this redeemer was actually looking for him and when told she would be the one to carry him, she believed. There were others that were looking also. John 1:

> 40 One of the two which heard John [the baptist] speak, and followed him, was Andrew, Simon Peter's brother.

> 41 He first findeth his own brother Simon, and saith unto him, We have found the Messias, which is, being interpreted, the Christ.

Joseph was also given information about Jesus when he was considering putting away Mary after finding out she was pregnant. Matthew 1:

> 19 Then Joseph her husband, being a just man, and not willing to make her a publick example, was minded to put her away privily.

> 20 But while he thought on these things, behold, the angel of the Lord appeared unto him in a dream, saying, Joseph, thou son of David, fear not to take unto thee Mary thy wife: for that which is conceived in her is of the Holy Ghost.

> 21 And she shall bring forth a son, and thou shalt call his name JESUS: for he shall save his people from their sins.

Jesus became the Word of God incarnate or the embodiment of God and His will on earth. His life represented God's will on earth. Whatever Jesus did was a reflection of what God wanted for mankind. John 8:

29 And he that sent me is with me: the Father hath not left me alone; for I do always those things that please him.

What were some of the things Jesus did? He healed the sick, raised the dead, cast out demons, and performed miracles. As he did this he was expressing the will of God to mankind. He also fulfilled the Law, even going to the cross and sacrificing his life for us to save us from our sins. Galatians gives us additional information about Jesus' accomplishments. Galatians 3

13 Christ hath redeemed us from the curse of the law, being made a curse for us: for it is written, Cursed is every one that hangeth on a tree:

I have always found it interesting when looking at the first recorded words of Jesus and his last recorded words just before he gave up his life. His first recorded words are found in the Gospel of Luke after Mary and Joseph find him after they discovered him missing.

Luke 24

46 And it came to pass, that after three days they found him in the temple, sitting in the midst of the doctors, both hearing them, and asking them questions.

47 And all that heard him were astonished at his understanding and answers.

48 And when they saw him, they were amazed: and his mother said unto him, Son, why hast thou thus dealt with us? behold, thy father and I have sought thee sorrowing.

> 49 And he said unto them, How is it that ye sought me? wist ye
> not that I must be about my Father's business?

Jesus knew why he was here. His last recorded words before his death are found in

John 19

> 30 When Jesus therefore had received the vinegar, he said, It
> is finished: and he bowed his head, and gave up the ghost.

What was finished? His father's work. Our redemption. Our remission of sins. Our pathway to salvation. It was all fulfilled in the finished work of Jesus.

I think the Gospel of John pretty much sums up the life of Jesus. John 21

> 25 And there are also many other things which Jesus did, the
> which, if they should be written every one, I suppose that
> even the world itself could not contain the books that should
> be written. Amen.

Upon the resurrection and subsequent ascending into heaven and Jesus' physical absence from the earth, the next administration began on the day of Pentecost and that is the administration of *Grace* which is the time in which we live.

Grace

In this administration of Grace in which we live our salvation, i.e. forgiveness of sins is not by our works. We find this in Ephesians 2

4 But God, who is rich in mercy, for his great love wherewith he loved us,

5 Even when we were dead in sins, hath quickened us together with Christ, (by grace ye are saved;)

6 And hath raised us up together, and made us sit together in heavenly places in Christ Jesus:

7 That in the ages to come he might shew the exceeding riches of his grace in his kindness toward us through Christ Jesus.

8 For by grace are ye saved through faith; and that not of yourselves: it is the gift of God:

9 Not of works, lest any man should boast.

This is good news. We or anyone for that matter can receive salvation, which is our way to heaven by grace. This is the result of the work and accomplishment that was done by Jesus for us. That is why no person can say, "Well certainly I'm going to heaven, after all, I'm a good person. I don't smoke, drink or swear. That's got to carry some weight with God." Well I think the book of Romans, I Corinthians and Galatians has something to say about that. Romans 3

20 Therefore by the deeds of the law there shall no flesh be justified in his sight: for by the law is the knowledge of sin.

I Corinthians 1

29 That no flesh should glory in his presence.

And Galatians 2

16 Knowing that a man is not justified by the works of the law,
but by the faith of Jesus Christ, even we have believed in
Jesus Christ, that we might be justified by the faith of Christ,
and not by the works of the law: for by the works of the law
shall no flesh be justified.

Now this may get the ire of some who think they can earn their
salvation. Many "religions" teach this, but they would be wrong.
Salvation is a "gift" from God as stated in Ephesians 2:8. A gift is a
gift and can't be earned. The only way you can be saved is found in

Romans 10: 9&10

9 That if thou shalt confess with thy mouth the Lord Jesus, and
shalt believe in thine heart that God hath raised him from
the dead, thou shalt be saved.

10 For with the heart man believeth unto righteousness; and
with the mouth confession is made unto salvation.

Because of the work of Jesus, all mankind can receive salvation,
eternal life, by confessing Jesus as lord and believing in their hearts
that God raise him from the dead. It is your choice. God did this for
mankind out of His love. You can either accept it or reject it. Look
what Jesus said in Luke 12

4 And I say unto you my friends, Be not afraid of them that
kill the body, and after that have no more that they can do.

5 But I will forewarn you whom ye shall fear: Fear him, which after he hath killed hath power to cast into hell; yea, I say unto you, Fear him.

Who do you think Jesus was talking about here? Obviously, Satan, the great deceiver. If he can get someone to reject Jesus then he has won, and that person will go to hell, not because he sinned, but because he rejected the savior from sin, Jesus. I know a number of people, wonderful kind giving people, who have not confessed Jesus as lord. These people sometimes live better lives than some Christians I know, but by not accepting Jesus as lord and the free gift of salvation will unfortunately be cast to hell. This is the adversary's whole intent as Jesus stated in John 10

9 I am the door: by me if any man enter in, he shall be saved, and shall go in and out, and find pasture.

10 The thief cometh not, but for to steal, and to kill, and to destroy: I am come that they might have life, and that they might have it more abundantly.

That's it!! Jesus came and gave his life so that we can live life to the fullest and not be beaten up by the adversary. Do you know that if the adversary had known about this administration he would never have had Jesus killed? Look at what it says in I Corinthians 2

7 But we speak the wisdom of God in a mystery, even the hidden wisdom, which God ordained before the world unto our glory:

8 Which none of the princes of this world knew: for had they known it, they would not have crucified the Lord of glory.

God in His wisdom never revealed this administration until the day of Pentecost with the first outpouring of His Holy Spirit born in a person, first the apostles and then about 3000 souls. Colossians tells us what the riches of the glory of this administration is in Colossians 1

> 27 To whom God would make known what is the riches of the glory of this mystery among the Gentiles; which is Christ in you, the hope of glory:

When you confess Jesus as Lord you become born again of incorruptible seed. I Peter 1:

> 23 Being born again, not of corruptible seed, but of incorruptible, by the word of God, which liveth and abideth for ever.

With this new birth and the gift of holy spirit you receive "Christ in you, the hope of glory". This was never available before in the history of mankind to receive Christ in you, incorruptible seed and the hope of eternal life. This gives us access to God that allows us to come to Him as His children. Hebrews 4

> 16 Let us therefore come boldly unto the throne of grace, that we may obtain mercy, and find grace to help in time of need.

Do you see what throne it is? It's the throne of *grace* that we go to. Not the throne of good works but of grace. And how are we to come to it with our needs? **BOLDLY!!!!!**

We are no longer little worm's that have to crawl up to God and beg, but we can come to Him boldly as son's because of the free gift He gives us at the time of salvation.

It is not the scope of this book to look into all that is available to us in this administration. There are good books available to help you in learning how to live in this administration. But suffice to say this administration can be summed up by looking at II Corinthians 3:

> 7 But if the [ad]ministration of death, written and engraven in stones, was glorious, so that the children of Israel could not stedfastly behold the face of Moses for the glory of his countenance; which glory was to be done away:

> 8 How shall not the[ad] ministration of the spirit be rather glorious?

> 9 For if the [ad]ministration of condemnation be glory, much more doth the [ad] ministration of righteousness exceed in glory.

> 10 For even that which was made glorious had no glory in this respect, by reason of the glory that excelleth.

> 11 For if that which is done away was glorious, much more that which remaineth is glorious.

> 12 Seeing then that we have such hope, we use great plainness of speech:

> 13 And not as Moses, which put a vail over his face, that the children of Israel could not stedfastly look to the end of that which is abolished:

> 14 But their minds were blinded: for until this day remaineth the same vail untaken away in the reading of the old testament;

which vail is done away in Christ.15 But even unto this day, when Moses is read, the vail is upon their heart.

16 Nevertheless when it shall turn to the Lord, the vail shall be taken away.

17 Now the Lord is that Spirit: and where the Spirit of the Lord is, there is liberty.

18 But we all, with open face beholding as in a glass the glory of the Lord, are changed into the same image from glory to glory, even as by the Spirit of the Lord.

This is referencing the time that Moses received the Ten Commandments mentioned in Exodus 34:19-25. Even though the administration of the Law was glorious it can't be compared to this administration. When well meaning Christians try to apply the law to this administration it is like putting a veil on their hearts because it denies the accomplishments of Christ. As we walk by the spirit and the liberty of Christ, we will be changed from glory to glory by the spirit of the Lord.

This administration will change abruptly with the coming of Christ for his saints and will usher in the Appearing or Revelation administration.

Appearing or Revelation

The onset of this administration will be a real game changer for mankind. It will be a time of great tribulation as recorded in Revelation. With the "gathering together" of the church, all born again believers, the rest of mankind will be left to deal with the adversary. Jesus said in John 9:

5 As long as I am in the world, I am the light of the world.

Even though Jesus ascended into heaven, as people became born again and received the gift of holy spirit, Christ in them, Jesus remained in the world and was the light of the world. Every born again Christian whether or not they know it, is a light in the world. At the gathering together all spiritual light will be removed and the adversary loosed. The promise of Jesus returning was made by the angels at the time of his accession as recorded in Acts1:

8 But ye shall receive power, after that the Holy Ghost is come upon you: and ye shall be witnesses unto me both in Jerusalem, and in all Judaea, and in Samaria, and unto the uttermost part of the earth.

9 And when he had spoken these things, while they beheld, he was taken up; and a cloud received him out of their sight.

10 And while they looked stedfastly toward heaven as he went up, behold, two men stood by them in white apparel;

11 Which also said, Ye men of Galilee, why stand ye gazing up into heaven? This same Jesus, which is taken up from you into heaven, shall so come in like manner as ye have seen him go into heaven.

This event is recorded in I and II Thessalonians and I Corinthians. Let's look at I Thessalonians 4:

13 But I would not have you to be ignorant, brethren, concerning them which are asleep, that ye sorrow not, even as others which have no hope.

14 For if we believe that Jesus died and rose again, even so them also which sleep in Jesus will God bring with him.

15 For this we say unto you by the word of the Lord, that we which are alive and remain unto the coming of the Lord shall not prevent them which are asleep.

16 For the Lord himself shall descend from heaven with a shout, with the voice of the archangel, and with the trump of God: and the dead in Christ shall rise first:

17 Then we which are alive and remain shall be caught up together with them in the clouds, to meet the Lord in the air: and so shall we ever be with the Lord.

God is telling the believers that He doesn't want them to be stupid regarding those loved ones who have died.

This event will start with God raising the dead believers first then we which are alive at the time of his coming will be "caught up" at the same time to meet Jesus in the air. There is a saying that goes, "you can't avoid death and taxes". Well I can tell you, you can get a good accountant and avoid taxes *and* you can get born again and avoid death if you are alive when Christ returns. This is why we are not like those others who have no hope. We get a little more insight into this in II Thessalonians 2:

1 Now we beseech you, brethren, by the coming of our Lord Jesus Christ, and by our gathering together unto him,

2 That ye be not soon shaken in mind, or be troubled, neither by spirit, nor by word, nor by letter as from us, as that the day of Christ is at hand.

DEAN J. SANDELL

3 Let no man deceive you by any means: for that day shall not come, except there come a falling away first, and that man of sin be revealed, the son of perdition;

4 Who opposeth and exalteth himself above all that is called God, or that is worshipped; so that he as God sitteth in the temple of God, shewing himself that he is God.

5 Remember ye not, that, when I was yet with you, I told you these things?

6 And now ye know what withholdeth that he might be revealed in his time.

7 For the mystery of iniquity doth already work: only he who now letteth will let, until he be taken out of the way.

8 And then shall that Wicked be revealed, whom the Lord shall consume with the spirit of his mouth, and shall destroy with the brightness of his coming:

9 Even him, whose coming is after the working of Satan with all power and signs and lying wonders,

10 And with all deceivableness of unrighteousness in them that perish; because they received not the love of the truth, that they might be saved.

11 And for this cause God shall send them strong delusion, that they should believe a lie:

12 That they all might be damned who believed not the truth, but had pleasure in unrighteousness.

This added information tells us that once the saints are "gathered together", taking all the "light" out of the world, then the "son of perdition" will be reveled, "whose coming is after the working of Satan with all power and signs and lying wonders, and with all deceivableness of unrighteousness in them that perish; because they received not the love of the truth, that they might be saved." This is the arrival of "the" antichrist whom men will worship as God. The reason that "the" antichrist cannot be reveled is because there is still "light" in the world. I John tells us that there are antichrist's in the world, 1 John 4:

> 3 And every spirit that confesseth not that Jesus Christ is come in the flesh is not of God: and this is that spirit of antichrist, whereof ye have heard that it should come; and even now already is it in the world.

Every religion that does not recognize Jesus as the Son of God is by default, "anti-Christ". However "the" antichrist is still in abeyance until the gathering together. Is he/she on the earth? I believe that he/she is because the adversary doesn't know when Christ is coming back any more than Christians do. It would stand then that he would have to have in place his person to be ready when Christ comes back. To try and guess who it might be, (although I have a few people in mind), just kidding, it would be foolish to speculate.

I would like to point out the word "rapture" is commonly used to refer to this event. However in I Thessalonians the term "caught up" is used and here the term "gathering together" is used. While there is not necessarily anything wrong with the word "rapture" I prefer to use the terms used in the Word and refer to it as the "gathering together". We can now look at additional information of what will take place at this time by looking at I Corinthians 15:

12 Now if Christ be preached that he rose from the dead, how say some among you that there is no resurrection of the dead?

13 But if there be no resurrection of the dead, then is Christ not risen:

14 And if Christ be not risen, then is our preaching vain, and your faith is also vain.

15 Yea, and we are found false witnesses of God; because we have testified of God that he raised up Christ: whom he raised not up, if so be that the dead rise not.

16 For if the dead rise not, then is not Christ raised:

17 And if Christ be not raised, your faith is vain; ye are yet in your sins.

18 Then they also which are fallen asleep in Christ are perished.

19 If in this life only we have hope in Christ, we are of all men most miserable.

20 But now is Christ risen from the dead, and become the firstfruits of them that slept.

21 For since by man came death, by man came also the resurrection of the dead.

22 For as in Adam all die, even so in Christ shall all be made alive.

23 But every man in his own order: Christ the firstfruits; afterward they that are Christ's at his coming.

24 Then cometh the end, when he shall have delivered up the kingdom to God, even the Father; when he shall have put down all rule and all authority and power.

25 For he must reign, till he hath put all enemies under his feet.

26 The last enemy that shall be destroyed is death.

Paul here is dealing with people that were saying that Christ is not risen, can we say antichrists? He is helping them to not be "ignorant" as he wrote to the Thessalonians'.

He then continues to answer the question of just how and what is going to happen. I Corinthians 15:

33 Be not deceived: evil communications corrupt good manners.

34 Awake to righteousness, and sin not; for some have not the knowledge of God: I speak this to your shame.

35 But some man will say, How are the dead raised up? and with what body do they come?

36 Thou fool, that which thou sowest is not quickened, except it die:

37 And that which thou sowest, thou sowest not that body that shall be, but bare grain, it may chance of wheat, or of some other grain:

38 But God giveth it a body as it hath pleased him, and to every seed his own body.

39 All flesh is not the same flesh: but there is one kind of flesh of men, another flesh of beasts, another of fishes, and another of birds.

40 There are also celestial bodies, and bodies terrestrial: but the glory of the celestial is one, and the glory of the terrestrial is another.

41 There is one glory of the sun, and another glory of the moon, and another glory of the stars: for one star differeth from another star in glory.

42 So also is the resurrection of the dead. It is sown in corruption; it is raised in incorruption:

43 It is sown in dishonour; it is raised in glory: it is sown in weakness; it is raised in power:

44 It is sown a natural body; it is raised a spiritual body. There is a natural body, and there is a spiritual body.

45 And so it is written, The first man Adam was made a living soul; the last Adam was made a quickening spirit.

46 Howbeit that was not first which is spiritual, but that which is natural; and afterward that which is spiritual.

47 The first man is of the earth, earthy: the second man is the Lord from heaven.

48 As is the earthy, such are they also that are earthy: and as is the heavenly, such are they also that are heavenly.

49 And as we have borne the image of the earthy, we shall also bear the image of the heavenly.

50 Now this I say, brethren, that flesh and blood cannot inherit the kingdom of God; neither doth corruption inherit incorruption.

51 Behold, I shew you a mystery; We shall not all sleep, but we shall all be changed,

52 In a moment, in the twinkling of an eye, at the last trump: for the trumpet shall sound, and the dead shall be raised incorruptible, and we shall be changed.

53 For this corruptible must put on incorruption, and this mortal must put on immortality.

54 So when this corruptible shall have put on incorruption, and this mortal shall have put on immortality, then shall be brought to pass the saying that is written, Death is swallowed up in victory.

55 O death, where is thy sting? O grave, where is thy victory?

56 The sting of death is sin; and the strength of sin is the law.

57 But thanks be to God, which giveth us the victory through our Lord Jesus Christ.

58 Therefore, my beloved brethren, be ye stedfast, unmoveable, always abounding in the work of the Lord, forasmuch as ye know that your labour is not in vain in the Lord.

DEAN I. SANDELL

WOW!!!! There is a lot in this section of scripture. But the bottom line is that at the return of Christ the dead will be changed first and then those who are alive will be changed, and together we will be with the Lord in the air. We will receive that same spiritual body that Jesus has.

So what happens when you die? It is clear that God is going to have to change a persons body to an incorruptible body like Jesus'. People who have died are then in a state of "awaiting" the return. Since the believers have to go meet Jesus in the air together, then the dead are simply awaiting the return in what the Word calls, sleep. Although a person is "asleep" awaiting the return, at the moment of death their next thought will be that of the gathering together. On the other hand for those who die without Christ, their next thought will be that of judgment.

These verses are to give us hope. For us who have believed, we will be gathered together to be with Jesus and God for eternity. Remember when I told you that Mary was looking for the Messiah and because of that, she believed and brought forth Jesus' first coming? Well, we as believers are to be "looking for" his return and second coming. Titus 2:

> 13 Looking for that blessed hope, and the glorious appearing of the great God and our Saviour Jesus Christ;

I think a lot of people are dreading the return, and I mean Christians, because they think they are going to get payback for how they lived. The truth is that we will be rewarded for our walk on earth. Since accepting Jesus as our Lord, our sins have all been forgiven. It's the unbelievers that will be judged for their non acceptance of Jesus and rejecting the savior from sin.

As I mentioned, after we have been gathered together, the rest of mankind will be going through the tribulation of revelation which we have been saved from.

This is told to us in I Thessalonians 1:

> 10 And to wait for his Son from heaven, whom he raised from the dead, even Jesus, which delivered us from the wrath to come.

I am a carpenter and many times after I finish a project I will hide a calling card saying when I did the job, who for, and then I will add the phrase, "has Christ come back yet?" so when someone years later remodels my work and finds it, it might peak their interest. I also think that if they read it, and he has returned, they're in a lot of trouble.

The end of this administration will be at the time of the Great White Throne judgment as recorded in Revelation 20:

> 10 And the devil that deceived them was cast into the lake of fire and brimstone, where the beast and the false prophet are, and shall be tormented day and night for ever and ever.

> 11 And I saw a great white throne, and him that sat on it, from whose face the earth and the heaven fled away; and there was found no place for them.

> 12 And I saw the dead, small and great, stand before God; and the books were opened: and another book was opened, which is the book of life: and the dead were judged out of those things which were written in the books, according to their works.

13 And the sea gave up the dead which were in it; and death and hell delivered up the dead which were in them: and they were judged every man according to their works.

14 And death and hell were cast into the lake of fire. This is the second death.

15 And whosoever was not found written in the book of life was cast into the lake of fire.

This is the appointed end for those who have rejected God along with the Devil and his angels. The Devil is very aware of his end. That is why he works overtime to deceive the nations and people. At the end of this administration, the final administration will be put in place and we will live forever with God and our Savior Jesus Christ. The final administration is the

Paradise Administration. God will re-establish His original intent from the time of Adam and Eve, for His children, to live in eternity.

Paradise

There are mentions of this new heaven and earth in Isaiah 65:

17 For, behold, I create new heavens and a new earth: and the former shall not be remembered, nor come into mind.

Also in Isaiah 66:

22 For as the new heavens and the new earth, which I will make, shall remain before me, saith the LORD, so shall your seed and your name remain.

And in II Peter 3:

> 9 The Lord is not slack concerning his promise, as some men count slackness; but is longsuffering to us-ward, not willing that any should perish, but that all should come to repentance.

> 10 But the day of the Lord will come as a thief in the night; in the which the heavens shall pass away with a great noise, and the elements shall melt with fervent heat, the earth also and the works that are therein shall be burned up.

> 11 Seeing then that all these things shall be dissolved, what manner of persons ought ye to be in all holy conversation and godliness,

> 12 Looking for and hasting unto the coming of the day of God, wherein the heavens being on fire shall be dissolved, and the elements shall melt with fervent heat?

> 13 Nevertheless we, according to his promise, look for new heavens and a new earth, wherein dwelleth righteousness.

God is longsuffering wanting none to perish. It will be quite a sight when this earth is dissolved and the new heaven and earth are brought forth. The final reference to this event is found in Revelation 21:

> 1 And I saw a new heaven and a new earth: for the first heaven and the first earth were passed away; and there was no more sea.

> 2 And I John saw the holy city, new Jerusalem, coming down from God out of heaven, prepared as a bride adorned for her husband.

3 And I heard a great voice out of heaven saying, Behold, the tabernacle of God is with men, and he will dwell with them, and they shall be his people, and God himself shall be with them, and be their God.

4 And God shall wipe away all tears from their eyes; and there shall be no more death, neither sorrow, nor crying, neither shall there be any more pain: for the former things are passed away.

5 And he that sat upon the throne said, Behold, I make all things new. And he said unto me, Write: for these words are true and faithful.

6 And he said unto me, It is done. I am Alpha and Omega, the beginning and the end. I will give unto him that is athirst of the fountain of the water of life freely.

This is our hope. The last verses of Revelation says some very important things

Revelation 22:

18 For I testify unto every man that heareth the words of the prophecy of this book, If any man shall add unto these things, God shall add unto him the plagues that are written in this book:

19 And if any man shall take away from the words of the book of this prophecy, God shall take away his part out of the book of life, and out of the holy city, and from the things which are written in this book.

20 He which testifieth these things saith, Surely I come quickly. Amen. Even so, come, Lord Jesus.

And finally, the last words of the Bible tell us in Revelation 22:

21 The grace of our Lord Jesus Christ be with you all. Amen.

We can now look into other keys to rightly dividing the Word of God.

CHAPTER 6

Scripture Buildup

S CRIPTURE BUILD UP is where one section of scripture gives only a part of the information and more information on the subject is given in another part of scripture. We saw this principal in the study of the administration of Appearing and Revelation. I Thessalonians combined with II Thessalonians and I Corinthians gave us a more complete understanding of the events that will take place. We can look at a couple of other examples and see this principal in action.

Simon of Cyrene

It is a common belief that Jesus carried his cross to Calvary. This is based primarily on a scripture found in the Gospel of John. John 19:

> 13 When Pilate therefore heard that saying, he brought Jesus forth, and sat down in the judgment seat in a place that is called the Pavement, but in the Hebrew, Gabbatha.

> 14 And it was the preparation of the passover, and about the sixth hour: and he saith unto the Jews, Behold your King!

> 15 But they cried out, Away with him, away with him, crucify him. Pilate saith unto them, Shall I crucify your King? The chief priests answered, We have no king but Caesar.

16 Then delivered he him therefore unto them to be crucified. And they took Jesus, and led him away.

17 And he bearing his cross went forth into a place called the place of a skull, which is called in the Hebrew Golgotha:

From this verse it would appear that Jesus bared the wooden cross. But as we look at other scriptures concerning this event, we will find out who really bared the cross and what cross Jesus really bore.

The other three Gospels also record this event and will give us added information regarding it. Matthew 27:

27 Then the soldiers of the governor took Jesus into the common hall, and gathered unto him the whole band of soldiers.

28 And they stripped him, and put on him a scarlet robe.

29 And when they had platted a crown of thorns, they put it upon his head, and a reed in his right hand: and they bowed the knee before him, and mocked him, saying, Hail, King of the Jews

30 And they spit upon him, and took the reed, and smote him on the head.

31 And after that they had mocked him, they took the robe off from him, and put his own raiment on him, and led him away to crucify him.

32 And as they came out, they found a man of Cyrene, Simon by name: him they compelled to bear his cross.

Jesus, who has just been beaten severely, was taken from the judgment hall by the Romans soldiers and just as they came out this man in town for the Passover, Simon of Cyrene, was pulled from the crowd and compelled to carry the cross. You will notice that it says they "compelled" him to carry the cross. I would suspect that you would not argue with a Roman soldier. Next is the Gospel of Mark. Mark 15:

16 And the soldiers led him away into the hall, called Praetorium; and they call together the whole band.

17 And they clothed him with purple, and platted a crown of thorns, and put it about his head,

18 And began to salute him, Hail, King of the Jews!

19 And they smote him on the head with a reed, and did spit upon him, and bowing their knees worshipped him.

20 And when they had mocked him, they took off the purple from him, and put his own clothes on him, and led him out to crucify him.

21 And they compel one Simon a Cyrenian, who passed by, coming out of the country, the father of Alexander and Rufus, to bear his cross.

22 And they bring him unto the place Golgotha, which is, being interpreted, The place of a skull.

Again, it is evident that as they led Jesus out Simon, who, as mentioned before, was in Jerusalem for the Passover, was just passing by and got caught up in this horrible event. Touching the cross, an instrument of death, just made him "unclean" for the Passover. The next gospel is Luke 23:

20 Pilate therefore, willing to release Jesus, spake again to them.

21 But they cried, saying, Crucify him, crucify him.

22 And he said unto them the third time, Why, what evil hath he done? I have found no cause of death in him: I will therefore chastise him, and let him go.

23 And they were instant with loud voices, requiring that he might be crucified. And the voices of them and of the chief priests prevailed.

24 And Pilate gave sentence that it should be as they required.

25 And he released unto them him that for sedition and murder was cast into prison, whom they had desired; but he delivered Jesus to their will.

26 And as they led him away, they laid hold upon one Simon, a Cyrenian, coming out of the country, and on him they laid the cross, that he might bear it after Jesus.

You could, from verse 25, conclude from "that he might bear it after Jesus" imply that "after" Jesus carried the cross for a while, then Simon carried it. This is not practical when comparing the other three gospels and the fact that by this time Jesus was probably being carried along by the soldiers because of the condition he was in.

So what was the cross Jesus bore? I Corinthians 1:

17 For Christ sent me not to baptize, but to preach the gospel: not with wisdom of words, lest the cross of Christ should be made of none effect.

18 For the preaching of the cross is to them that perish foolishness; but unto us which are saved it is the power of God.

This "cross of Christ" and the "preaching of the cross" certainly can't be referring to the wooden cross. Crucifixion was a common means of execution in those times. It has to be another cross. I Peter 2:

24 Who his own self bare our sins in his own body on the tree, that we, being dead to sins, should live unto righteousness: by whose stripes ye were healed.

It is what Jesus did for us on the wooden cross of bearing our sins for us. That was the cross he bore. He took the iniquity of our sins and paid the price for us. His cross was to do the Fathers' will and give his life for us. Ephesians 2:

15 Having abolished in his flesh the enmity, even the law of commandments contained in ordinances; for to make in himself of twain one new man, so making peace;

16 And that he might reconcile both unto God in one body by the cross, having slain the enmity thereby:

17 And came and preached peace to you which were afar off, and to them that were nigh.

18 For through him we both have access by one Spirit unto the Father.

19 Now therefore ye are no more strangers and foreigners, but fellowcitizens with the saints, and of the household of God;

20 And are built upon the foundation of the apostles and prophets, Jesus Christ himself being the chief corner stone;

21 In whom all the building fitly framed together growth unto an holy temple in the Lord:

22 In whom ye also are builded together for an habitation of God through the Spirit.

It is the cross that Christ bore that gives us access to our Father, God. Pictures of Jesus caring the cross my make for good religious stories and tradition, but flies in the face of the accuracy of God's Word. We can now look at another event regarding the crucifixion buy using the same principal of scripture build up.

The Others Crucified With Jesus

It is commonly believed that there were only two others crucified with Jesus. If we use the principal of scripture build up we will discover that that is not the case. As we look into the others crucified with Jesus I want to look at two words that will be used in our study. Jesus used these words in John 10:

1 Verily, verily, I say unto you, He that entereth not by the door into the sheepfold, but climbeth up some other way, the same is a thief and a robber.

It would seem that a "thief" and a "robber" would be the same thing. However by looking at the Greek words used it becomes apparent that they aren't. The word for thief is the word "*kleptes*", which means, one who uses craft. The word for robber is "*lestes*", which means, one who uses violence. Another word used in the account of the crucifixion is the word "malefactors" found in Luke 23:32. A malefactor is simply an evildoer. That word is the word "kakourgoi". This becomes important as we get into our study. Let's start by looking at the account found in Matthew 27:

33 And when they were come unto a place called Golgotha, that is to say, a place of a skull,

34 They gave him vinegar to drink mingled with gall: and when he had tasted thereof, he would not drink.

35 And they crucified him, and parted his garments, casting lots: that it might be fulfilled which was spoken by the prophet, They parted my garments among them, and upon my vesture did they cast lots.

36 And sitting down they watched him there;

37 And set up over his head his accusation written, THIS IS JESUS THE KING OF THE JEWS.

38 Then were there two thieves crucified with him, one on the right hand, and another on the left.

39 And they that passed by reviled him, wagging their heads.

40 And saying, Thou that destroyest the temple, and buildest it in three days, save thyself. If thou be the Son of God, come down from the cross.

41 Likewise also the chief priests mocking him, with the scribes and elders, said,

42 He saved others; himself he cannot save. If he be the King of Israel, let him now come down from the cross, and we will believe him.

43 He trusted in God; let him deliver him now, if he will have him: for he said, I am the Son of God.

44 The thieves also, which were crucified with him, cast the same in his teeth.

The word used here for "thieves" is the Greek word "lestai", a form of the word "lestes" which is "one who uses violence. We should also notice that both the thieves joined in with the chief priests and the scribes and elders in mocking him. Looking at verses 45 through 50 we gain added insight. Mathew 27:

45 Now from the sixth hour there was darkness over all the land unto the ninth hour.

46 And about the ninth hour Jesus cried with a loud voice, saying, Eli, Eli, lama sabachthani? that is to say, My God, my God, why hast thou forsaken me?

47 Some of them that stood there, when they heard that, said, This man calleth for Elias.

48 And straightway one of them ran, and took a spunge, and filled it with vinegar, and put it on a reed, and gave him to drink.

49 The rest said, Let be, let us see whether Elias will come to save him.

50 Jesus, when he had cried again with a loud voice, yielded up the ghost.

From these verses we get a timeline. In Jewish time reckoning the sixth hour was from 12pm to 1pm. The ninth hour was 3pm to 4pm. We see here that for about 3 hours there was darkness in the land. The next gospel is Mark 15:

21 And they compel one Simon a Cyrenian, who passed by, coming out of the country, the father of Alexander and Rufus, to bear his cross.

22 And they bring him unto the place Golgotha, which is, being interpreted, The place of a skull.

23 And they gave him to drink wine mingled with myrrh: but he received it not.

24 And when they had crucified him, they parted his garments, casting lots upon them, what every man should take.

25 And it was the third hour, and they crucified him.

26 And the superscription of his accusation was written over, THE KING OF THE JEWS.

27 And with him they crucify two thieves; the one on his right hand, and the other on his left.

28 And the scripture was fulfilled, which saith, And he was numbered with the transgressors.

29 And they that passed by railed on him, wagging their heads, and saying, Ah, thou that destroyest the temple, and buildest it in three days,

30 Save thyself, and come down from the cross.

31 Likewise also the chief priests mocking said among themselves with the scribes, He saved others; himself he cannot save.

32 Let Christ the King of Israel descend now from the cross, that we may see and believe. And they that were crucified with him reviled him.

As we have all ready learned Simon of Cyrene was compelled to carry the cross. Not much is added here except that the hour of Jesus' crucifixion is set. He was crucified at the third hour which was 9am to 10am. This tells us that Jesus hung on the cross from approximately 9am to 3pm a total of about 6 hours. Also note that Mark again mentions that, "they that were crucified with him reviled him." The next gospel is Luke 23:

32 And there were also two other, malefactors, led with him to be put to death.

33 And when they were come to the place, which is called Calvary, there they crucified him, and the malefactors, one on the right hand, and the other on the left.

34 Then said Jesus, Father, forgive them; for they know not what they do. And they parted his raiment, and cast lots.

35 And the people stood beholding. And the rulers also with them derided him, saying, He saved others; let him save himself, if he be Christ, the chosen of God.

36 And the soldiers also mocked him, coming to him, and offering him vinegar,

37 And saying, If thou be the king of the Jews, save thyself.

38 And a superscription also was written over him in letters of Greek, and Latin, and Hebrew, THIS IS THE KING OF THE JEWS.

39 And one of the malefactors which were hanged railed on him, saying, If thou be Christ, save thyself and us.

40 But the other answering rebuked him, saying, Dost not thou fear God, seeing thou art in the same condemnation?

41 And we indeed justly; for we receive the due reward of our deeds: but this man hath done nothing amiss.

42 And he said unto Jesus, Lord, remember me when thou comest into thy kingdom.

43 And Jesus said unto him, Verily I say unto thee, To day shalt thou be with me in paradise.

44 And it was about the sixth hour, and there was a darkness over all the earth until the ninth hour.

45 And the sun was darkened, and the veil of the temple was rent in the midst.

46 And when Jesus had cried with a loud voice, he said, Father, into thy hands I commend my spirit: and having said thus, he gave up the ghost.

Verse 32 gives us some new added information. It tells us that two "malefactors" were led with him. Remember that a malefactor is an "evil doer" and is the word, kakourgoi, not lestai as used in the other gospels. One very important thing to note here is that only one malefactor reviled Jesus and the other didn't, while the other two gospels mention that "both" reviled Jesus. Let's look at the gospel of John chapter 19. There is much mentioned in this chapter that is mentioned in the other gospels, so we will focus on the verses pertinent to our study of the crucifixion. John 19:

17 And he bearing his cross went forth into a place called the place of a skull, which is called in the Hebrew Golgotha:

18 Where they crucified him, and two other with him, on either side one, and Jesus in the midst.

There is an important word used in verse 18 and that is the word "midst". Grammatically, a person cannot be in the "midst" of two. They would be in the middle. However, when there are more than two a person would be in the "midst. The other word to note is the word, "other". In the Greek there are two words used for "other". One is "allos" and is used when there is a second of two and where there may be more. We could say it like this, "there were other players on the field" which would indicate that there were more than two. The other word used for "other" is "heteros" which is used when only two are involved. We would say, "there was the other player on the field" meaning there were only two. The word used in verse 18 is "allos" meaning more than two. Next let's look at John 19:

31 The Jews therefore, because it was the preparation, that the bodies should not remain upon the cross on the Sabbath day, (for that Sabbath day was an high day,) besought Pilate that their legs might be broken, and that they might be taken away.

32 Then came the soldiers, and brake the legs of the first, and of the other which was crucified with him.

33 But when they came to Jesus, and saw that he was dead already, they brake not his legs.

As the soldiers came to speed things up by breaking the legs of the ones crucified, they broke the legs of the first, then the legs of the second, *then* came to Jesus and saw that he was already dead. According to tradition, they would have broken the legs of the first, walked past Jesus, broke the legs of the other one and then go back to take care of Jesus only to find he was already dead which would make no sense. The other thing that needs to be noted is that the word "other" used here is the word, "allos" indicating more than two.

So from our study we can see that there were actually four crucified with Jesus and not two. The accuracy of the Word of God when it is rightly divided thrills the heart. We have to forsake religion and traditions and search the Word for it accuracy. This principal of, scripture build up, can also be used in the study of the day Jesus died, but that is for another time. We can now look at some more keys and principals to rightly dividing the Word.

CHAPTER 7

A Word Or Words Must Be Understood In Light Of Their Biblical Meaning

WHEN READING THE Bible, particularly the King James Version, it must be remembered that it was in Old English a long time ago. So words that were used then, may have a different meaning then today. We also have to understand that man has corrupted words over time so that they don't carry the original meaning that they use to. We can look at a few examples, one can be found in Luke 17:

> 7 But which of you, having a servant plowing or feeding cattle, will say unto him by and by, when he is come from the field, Go and sit down to meat?

> 8 And will not rather say unto him, Make ready wherewith I may sup, and gird thyself, and serve me, till I have eaten and drunken; and afterward thou shalt eat and drink?

> 9 Doth he thank that servant because he did the things that were commanded him? I trow not.

The phrase, "I trow not", meant, "I think or imagine not"

Psalm 88 and I Thessalonians 4 use the word "prevent". Psalm 88:

13 But unto thee have I cried, O LORD; and in the morning shall my prayer prevent thee.

I Thessalonians 4:

15 For this we say unto you by the word of the Lord, that we which are alive and remain unto the coming of the Lord shall not prevent them which are asleep.

In our vernacular today the word "prevent" means to hinder or stop someone or thing.

In the time that it was used in the Bible it means to "go before or proceed"

Another, odd word, if you will, is the word "letteth" found in I Thessalonians 2:

5 Remember ye not, that, when I was yet with you, I told you these things?

6 And now ye know what withholdeth that he might be revealed in his time.

7 For the mystery of iniquity doth already work: only he who now letteth will let, until he be taken out of the way.

We would understand the word today to mean, "allowing something to happen". However, at the time that it was used then it meant, "to withhold or hinder" as can be seen by the use of the word "withholdeth" in verse 6.

Another word that is misused is the word "temple". Specifically, regarding a person born again. They are reminded, "remember your body is the temple of the holy ghost" and reference the verse found in I Corinthians 6:

> 19 What? know ye not that your body is the temple of the Holy Ghost which is in you, which ye have of God, and ye are not your own?

But is that an accurate usage of that word? Look at what Peter had to say about himself as he was aware that his passing was approaching II Peter 1:

> 13 Yea, I think it meet, as long as I am in this tabernacle, to stir you up by putting you in remembrance;
>
> 14 Knowing that shortly I must put off this my tabernacle, even as our Lord Jesus Christ hath shewed me.

He is referring to his body as a "tabernacle" not a temple. We also see this reference found in II Corinthians 5:

> 1 For we know that if our earthly house of this tabernacle were dissolved, we have a building of God, an house not made with hands, eternal in the heavens.
>
> 4 For we that are in this tabernacle do groan, being burdened: not for that we would be unclothed, but clothed upon, that mortality might be swallowed up of life.

Another verse that will shed some light on this is found in II Corinthians 4:

> 7 But we have this treasure in earthen vessels, that the excellency of the power may be of God, and not of us.

It is clear that our earthly body is the "tabernacle" of God and not the temple. So what is the difference, and what is Paul referring to when he says, "know ye not that your body is the temple of the Holy Ghost"? First we need to understand what a tabernacle was in the Old Testament. According to Wikipedia, "The Tabernacle, according to the Hebrew Bible, was the portable earthly dwelling place for the Shekhinah from the time of the Exodus from Egypt through the conquering of the land of Canaan". This would make sense since it is a "portable" dwelling place. A temple on the other hand is a permanent structure which could house a tabernacle. So what was Paul saying when he referred to their body as a temple? Let's see to whom Paul was writing. II Corinthians 1:

> 1 Paul, an apostle of Jesus Christ by the will of God, and Timothy our brother, unto the church of God which is at Corinth, with all the saints which are in all Achaia:

It is clear that he was writing to the "church" and to "all the saints", a body of believers. So when he told them that your "body" is the "temple" of the Holy Ghost he was obviously referring to the collective "body" of believers at Corinth not a single individual which would be a tabernacle.

So, understanding that a word might have a different meaning today than when it was used years ago, will give us a better understanding of the Bible.

I think that two of the most misused words in the Bible are the words, "create" and "hope". Politician's promise that if elected they will "create" jobs. Scientists declare that they can now "create" life in a test tube. An actress will claim that she has "created" a new line of beauty aids. Well there is just one problem with that. They all had to start with something that already existed.

Biblically, the word "creates" means, "to bring into existence something that never existed before." The first usage of the word create is found in the first verse of the Bible. Genesis 1:

> 1 In the beginning God created the heaven and the earth.

> 2 And the earth was without form, and void; and darkness was upon the face of the deep. And the Spirit of God moved upon the face of the waters.

Accurately the verse should read, "God in the beginning created the heavens and the earth", because God is always first and the source of all things". It then goes on to say, "and the earth was without form, and void; and darkness was upon the face of the deep." If you were God would you "create" something that was, without form and void?

The book of Isaiah clears this up for us. Isaiah 45:

> 18 For thus saith the LORD that created the heavens; God himself that formed the earth and made it; he hath established it, he created it not in vain, he formed it to be inhabited: I am the LORD; and there is none else.

How many times do you think the word, create, or a form of it is used in the first few chapters of Genesis? One time, seven times, ten times, more? Preachers preach that the first chapter of Genesis is the account of God creating the heavens and earth. They say that on the first day God, "created light", on the second day He "created" the firmaments and divided the waters, and so on. But is that what it really says? Let's look at a few of these scriptures. Genesis 1:

> 3 And God said, Let there be light: and there was light.

6 And God said, Let there be a firmament in the midst of the waters, and let it divide the waters from the waters.

9 And God said, Let the waters under the heaven be gathered together unto one place, and let the dry land appear: and it was so.

11 And God said, Let the earth bring forth grass, the herb yielding seed, and the fruit tree yielding fruit after his kind, whose seed is in itself, upon the earth: and it was so.

Do you see a recurring pattern here? It states, "and God said let there be…." and ends with, "and "it was so". The reason God didn't have to "create", was because He was dealing with the substance that He had already created in the beginning. So how many times is the form of the word create used? The word "created" is used of three acts of creation the rest refer to these three acts. First He "created" the heavens and earth, then He "created" great whales and third He "created" man in His own image.

The question has to be asked, did God create Adam and Eve? Let's see what it says in Genesis 2:

7 And the LORD God formed man of the dust of the ground, and breathed into his nostrils the breath of life; and man became a living soul.

21 And the LORD God caused a deep sleep to fall upon Adam, and he slept: and he took one of his ribs, and closed up the flesh instead thereof;

22 And the rib, which the LORD God had taken from man, made he a woman, and brought her unto the man.

23 And Adam said, This is now bone of my bones, and flesh of my flesh: she shall be called Woman, because she was taken out of Man.

It is apparent from these verses that God used an existing substance, dirt, and formed man. He then used an existing substance, Adams rib, to make a woman. So what is the answer to the question, did God create Adam and Eve? We will start by looking at Genesis 1:

26 And God said, Let us make man in our image, after our likeness: and let them have dominion over the fish of the sea, and over the fowl of the air, and over the cattle, and over all the earth, and over every creeping thing that creepeth upon the earth.

27 So God created man in his own image, in the image of God created he him; male and female created he them.

To find out the image of God we need to go to the Gospel of John 4:

24 God is a Spirit: and they that worship him must worship him in spirit and in truth.

I think it states it quite clearly, that God the creator of the heavens and earth is a spirit, while man is flesh and bone. Adam made that clear when he said, "This is now bone of my bones, and flesh of my flesh: she shall be called Woman, because she was taken out of Man."

So what did God create? He created, brought into existence something that didn't exist before, spirit, and placed it on Adam and Eve. Why? So that He could talk and fellowship with them. Flesh and bone cannot communicate with spirit unless there is spirit upon an individual. That is why God had to create spirit so they could communicate. But it was upon a condition. That condition is found in Genesis 2:

> 16 And the LORD God commanded the man, saying, Of every tree of the garden thou mayest freely eat:

> 17 But of the tree of the knowledge of good and evil, thou shalt not eat of it: for in the day that thou eatest thereof thou shalt surely die.There were no if's and's or but's about it. You will surely die. When Adam and Eve sinned did they die? Obviously not. So what did? The spirit connection they had. It was now gone. Adam and Eve were now simply flesh and blood.

What about the times that we live in. Is God doing any more creating? Ephesians2:

> 8 For by grace are ye saved through faith; and that not of yourselves: it is the gift of God:

> 9 Not of works, lest any man should boast.

> 10 For we are his workmanship, created in Christ Jesus unto good works, which God hath before ordained that we should walk in them.

At the time of the new birth, holy spirit is created in us. We find out what happens to us when we become born again in II Corinthians 5:

> 17 Therefore if any man be in Christ, he is a new creature: old things are passed away; behold, all things are become new.

The Gospel to the Colossians as we have seen before gives us some very valuable information about this new creation Colossians 1:

27 To whom God would make known what is the riches of the glory of this mystery among the Gentiles; which is Christ in you, the hope of glory:

When you get born again by confessing Jesus as Lord, God, "creates" in you a new creation, His gift of holy spirit. It did not exist before the time of your new birth so it is a new creation.

There are some who say, "you are a spirit, you have a soul and live in a body", and when you get born again your spirit is recreated or that you have a recreated spirit. This cannot be true, if the usage of the word for create is accurate. If you had a spirit to begin with then it can't be "recreated". Man, become "body, soul and spirit" at the time of the new birth. Up until that time a person is simply body and soul.

I want to look at another misused and misunderstood word from the Bible and that is the word "hope." People use the word "hope" in the sense of wishful thinking. "I sure hope I can get a new car or I hope I can get a raise" or whatever else they may be desiring. However, we will see that biblical hope is the anticipation of a future event that *will* happen.

One of the most quoted verses in the Bible on hope is found in Hebrews 11:

1 Now faith is the substance of things hoped for, the evidence of things not seen.

Faith and hope work together. Hope is the "thing" desired, the "anticipated" result, while faith is the expectation of the "hope" coming to pass. It takes faith or believing to bring to pass the hope. Hope that is based on the promises of God and the "believing" that they will come to pass is what brings things to pass. This works in

DEAN J. SANDELL

both the positive side and the negative side. Hope in something bad alone will not necessarily bring it to pass, but believing that it will happen will eventually bring it to pass. This is what happened to Job. Job 3:

> 25 For the thing which I greatly feared is come upon me, and that which I was afraid of is come unto me.

If you don't know the account of Job, he lost everything because of a fear he had and in "faith" he acted upon it. Job 1:

> 1 There was a man in the land of Uz, whose name was Job; and that man was perfect and upright, and one that feared God, and eschewed evil.

> 2 And there were born unto him seven sons and three daughters.

> 3 His substance also was seven thousand sheep, and three thousand camels, and five hundred yoke of oxen, and five hundred she asses, and a very great household; so that this man was the greatest of all the men of the east.

> 4 And his sons went and feasted in their houses, every one his day; and sent and called for their three sisters to eat and to drink with them.

> 5 And it was so, when the days of their feasting were gone about, that Job sent and sanctified them, and rose up early in the morning, and offered burnt offerings according to the number of them all: for Job said, It may be that my sons have sinned, and cursed God in their hearts. Thus did Job continually.

What we see here is a man that was obviously blessed by God. However, he had one shortcoming. He was fearful that his children were sinning against God. He says in verse 5, "It may be that my sons have sinned, and cursed God in their hearts". He wasn't even really sure, but out of fear he offered burnt offerings for them. He was "hoping" that by doing this he was sanctifying them, in essence protecting them. But it was rooted in fear and he received the end results of his fear. You will notice, thus did Job continually. God did not ask him to do this, it was a fabrication on Job's part.

Now let's look at what can be accomplished when we apply faith and hope on the positive side. Romans 4:

17 (As it is written, I have made thee a father of many nations,) before him whom he believed, even God, who quickeneth the dead, and calleth those things which be not as though they were.

18 Who against hope believed in hope, that he might become the father of many nations, according to that which was spoken, So shall thy seed be.

19 And being not weak in faith, he considered not his own body now dead, when he was about an hundred years old, neither yet the deadness of Sara's womb:

20 He staggered not at the promise of God through unbelief; but was strong in faith, giving glory to God;

21 And being fully persuaded that, what he had promised, he was able also to perform.

Abraham wanted an heir, a son. So God made a promise to him, "I have made thee a father of many nations". However there was just one problem, Abraham and his wife, particularly his wife, were past child bearing age. But he had a promise from God that He would make him the father of many nations. So what did Abraham do? "Who against hope believed in hope". "And being not weak in faith, he considered not his own body now dead, when he was about an hundred years old, neither yet the deadness of Sara's womb".

I have heard that one translation of this verse stated it as this, "and being not weak in faith, he considered his own body now dead, when he was about an hundred years old, and the deadness of Sara's womb". Wouldn't it make sense that he was no fool and would have taken his circumstances into consideration? But what did he do? *He staggered not at the promise of God through unbelief; but was strong in faith, giving glory to God; And being fully persuaded that, what he had promised, he was able also to perform.* He maintained sight of his hope and was strong in faith. He had an expected outcome and based it on the promise that God had given him. He was also fully persuaded that what God had promised He was also able to perform. God's Word is full of promises that if we will take a promise, a hope, and believe, have an expectation of it being fulfilled it will come to pass because God's willingness equals His ability.

Look what Jesus said in Matthew 21:

> 22 And all things, whatsoever ye shall ask in prayer, believing, ye shall receive.

The "things" are your hope. Anything that you pray for, as long as it lines up with the Word and you "believe", have an expectation of receiving, you "shall" (absolutely) receive it.

A word about the word, believe. Believing is simply an expectation. Job had an "expectation" of something happening to his children if he didn't make these offerings. It was based in fear and he received the results. Abraham also had an expectation but instead of offering some self designed ritual, he, "against hope believed in hope." Proverbs 13:

> 12 Hope deferred maketh the heart sick: but when the desire cometh, it is a tree of life.

There are times that as you are awaiting the manifestation of what you are hoping for, you might get discouraged. But that is where your full persuasion has to kick in. That is what Abraham did. Did Jesus have hope? Hebrews 12:

> 2 Looking unto Jesus the author and finisher of our faith; who for the joy that was set before him endured the cross, despising the shame, and is set down at the right hand of the throne of God.

God showed Jesus what his sacrifice would do. He had to give Jesus a glimpse of what his accomplishment would do for mankind so that Jesus would have the courage to carry out his mission. It was the joy that Jesus received that helped him to offer himself for mankind. This is the same with us. We need to have a hope of something to keep us going. Remember, it is not wishful thinking but an anticipation of our desire coming to pass.

As believers we have the "hope" of Christ return. Colossians 1:

> 27 To whom God would make known what is the riches of the glory of this mystery among the Gentiles; which is Christ in you, the hope of glory.

The "hope of glory", which is the return of Christ and our living in eternity, is what gives us strength to live in the times that we live in. 1 Corinthians 13:

> 13 And now abideth faith, hope, charity, these three; but the greatest of these is charity.

We need all three to live the life Jesus came and gave his life for.

Before we close this subject I think it is important to look at another word and the phrase, "the fear of the Lord". This phrase is found primarily in the Old Testament but there are also some usages in the new. The first thing you have to understand about the word "fear" in this reference is not "to be afraid of". Since God is love, the last thing He would want us to do is, "be afraid of" Him. Love and fear cannot dwell in the same place. 1 John 4:

> 18 There is no fear in love; but perfect love casteth out fear: because fear hath torment. He that feareth is not made perfect in love.

The meaning of "fear" when used in "fear of the Lord" is actually meant, "to have reverence for" or "a deep respect for". It would stand to reason that since God is God we should have a reverential respect or awe of God, but hardly be afraid of Him. Proverbs 1:

> 7 The fear of the LORD is the beginning of knowledge: but fools despise wisdom and instruction.

To have a reverence for God is the beginning. Fools despise wisdom and instruction because they have no respect for God which makes them fools. Proverbs 14:

26 In the fear of the LORD is strong confidence: and his children shall have a place of refuge.

This could hardly mean that being afraid of God would give us strong confidence, since fear does just the opposite and makes one cower. Romans 3:

10 As it is written, There is none righteous, no, not one:

11 There is none that understandeth, there is none that seeketh after God.

12 They are all gone out of the way, they are together become unprofitable; there is none that doeth good, no, not one.

13 Their throat is an open sepulchre; with their tongues they have used deceit; the poison of asps is under their lips:

14 Whose mouth is full of cursing and bitterness:

15 Their feet are swift to shed blood:

16 Destruction and misery are in their ways:

17 And the way of peace have they not known:

18 There is no fear of God before their eyes.

These verses explains to us a lot of why the world is in the condition it is in. All these things mentioned in verses 11-17 is summed up in, "there is no fear of God before their eyes." When you have no reverence for God you become god unto yourself and since man is a fallen creature then the end result will be depravity. 2 Corinthians 7:

1 Having therefore these promises, dearly beloved, let us cleanse ourselves from all filthiness of the flesh and spirit, perfecting holiness in the fear of God.

This is what God has called us to, to cleanse ourselves from all filthiness of the flesh and spirit, perfecting holiness in the fear [reverence] of God. God is our loving heavenly father and the last thing He wants His children to be, would to be afraid of Him. He is truly worthy of our love and reverence for Him.

So we can see, that to have a good understanding of the Bible we must recognize the importance of understanding words in light of their biblical usage.

CHAPTER 8

Informational, Instructional and Result Verses

Informational

SOME VERSES IN the Bible give us information. One such verse gives us information on God's primary will for our lives. III John

> 2 Beloved, I wish [desire] above all things that thou mayest prosper and be in health, even as thy soul prospereth.

That's some very vital information to have. God is concerned about every aspect of our lives and has our best interest in mind. Let's look at Psalms 56:

> 9 When I cry unto thee, then shall mine enemies turn back: this I know; for God is for me.

That's something good to know, God is for me. Numbers 23:

> 19 God is not a man, that he should lie; neither the son of man, that he should repent: hath he said, and shall he not do it? or hath he spoken, and shall he not make it good?

It's good to know that God cannot lie, this is also found in Titus 1:

2 In hope of eternal life, which God, that cannot lie, promised before the world began;

How about I John 1:

5 This then is the message which we have heard of him, and declare unto you, that God is light, and in him is no darkness at all.

So when someone attributes evil to God we know from this verse that they are wrong.

I John 4:

8 He that loveth not knoweth not God; for God is love.

This would be a good starting point in studying the Bible. So you can see that you can learn a lot from informational scriptures.

Instructional

Instructional verses do just that, they instruct us. 1 Peter 5:

6 Humble yourselves therefore under the mighty hand of God, that he may exalt you in due time:

7 Casting all your care upon him; for he careth for you.

Here we are instructed to take an action, humbling ourselves under the mighty hand of God by casting all our care upon him. This is an action that we have to make a decision to do.

Romans 14:

> 19 Let us therefore follow after the things which make for peace, and things wherewith one may edify another.

When you see the word "let" it is telling us that this is something that we have to do. It is by a deliberate decision of our will to do it. Philippians 2:

> 5 Let this mind be in you, which was also in Christ Jesus:

How do we let the mind that was in Christ Jesus, be in us? First you have to go to the Word and discover how Jesus walked and talked. You would have to learn of him through studying primarily the Gospels and how he behaved. Then when you are faced with a situation you can put the kind of thoughts he had in your mind and walk in the same victories he did. Let's look at a couple of other verses that instruct us to "put on" Ephesians 4:

> 24 And that ye put on the new man, which after God is created in righteousness and true holiness.

Colossians 3:

> 10 And have put on the new man, which is renewed in knowledge after the image of him that created him:

Colossians 3:

> 12 Put on therefore, as the elect of God, holy and beloved, bowels of mercies, kindness, humbleness of mind, meekness, longsuffering;

13 Forbearing one another, and forgiving one another, if any man have a quarrel against any: even as Christ forgave you, so also do ye.

14 And above all these things put on charity, which is the bond of perfectness.

15 And let the peace of God rule in your hearts, to the which also ye are called in one body; and be ye thankful.

We are told in verse 12 to "put on", bowels of mercies, kindness, humbleness of mind, meekness, longsuffering. Then in verse 13 we are instructed of the "how" to do it. Forbearing one another, and forgiving one another, if any man have a quarrel against any: even as Christ forgave you, so also do ye. Verse 14, And above all these things put on charity, which is the bond of perfectness. These are all actions that we by the renewing of our minds can do. In verse 15 we are instructed to, "let the peace of God rule in your hearts" and "be ye thankful". These instructional verse will help us to be in "health" and "prosper".

Results

Some verses will instruct us and provide us with a result if we will do it. Proverbs 3:

5 Trust in the LORD with all thine heart; and lean not unto thine own understanding.

6 In all thy ways acknowledge him, and he shall direct thy paths.

7 Be not wise in thine own eyes: fear the LORD, and depart from evil.

8 It shall be health to thy navel, and marrow to thy bones.

As a result of trusting God, not leaning to our own understanding, and acknowledging Him, He will direct out paths. By not being wise in our own eyes, fear [respect, reverence] God and depart from evil the result will be health to our navel and marrow to our bones. In other words, it will produce a healthy life. Let's look at another scripture. Psalms 37:

> 3 Trust in the LORD, and do good; so shalt thou dwell in the land, and verily thou shalt be fed.

> 4 Delight thyself also in the LORD; and he shall give thee the desires of thine heart.

> 5 Commit thy way unto the LORD; trust also in him; and he shall bring it to pass.

> 6 And he shall bring forth thy righteousness as the light, and thy judgment as the noonday.

Verse 3 tells us that if we trust in the Lord, we will dwell in the land and be fed. This is God indicating to us that He will take care of us if we will trust in Him. That's the kind of God I want to have. We are then told in verse 4 to "delight" ourselves in the Lord and He will give us the "desires" of our hearts. The desires of our hearts may not always be godly. However if we will delight ourselves in Him, He will actually give us desires, Godly desires. And then all we have to do is commit our way, trust in Him and He will bring them to pass. Let's look at Gods instruction to us on prayer and the result we can get. Philippians 4:

DEAN J. SANDELL

6 Be careful [anxious] for nothing; but in every thing by prayer and supplication with thanksgiving let your requests be made known unto God.

7 And the peace of God, which passeth all understanding, shall keep your hearts and minds through Christ Jesus.

When we pray we are not to become "anxious" or stressed. We are to present our prayers and supplications to God with thanksgiving and the end result will be, *the peace of God, which passeth all understanding, shall keep your hearts and minds through Christ Jesus.* Philippians 4:

8 Finally, brethren, whatsoever things are true, whatsoever things are honest, whatsoever things are just, whatsoever things are pure, whatsoever things are lovely, whatsoever things are of good report; if there be any virtue, and if there be any praise, think on these things.

9 Those things, which ye have both learned, and received, and heard, and seen in me, do: and the God of peace shall be with you.

In verse 8 we are again instructed as to what to think. Things that are, true, honest, just, pure, lovely, good report, virtue and praise. Verse 9 then tells us to do it and the result will be, *the God of peace shall be with you.*

II Peter gives us the reason why we need to know these things. II Peter 1:

2 Grace and peace be multiplied unto you through the knowledge of God, and of Jesus our Lord,

3 According as his divine power hath given unto us all things that pertain unto life and godliness, through the knowledge of him that hath called us to glory and virtue:

4 Whereby are given unto us exceeding great and precious promises: that by these ye might be partakers of the divine nature, having escaped the corruption that is in the world through lust.

It is through a knowledge of God and Jesus that grace and peace are multiplied to us. God has given us by His divine power all things that pertain unto life and godliness, nothing is left out. But, this is only accomplished through a knowledge, and might I add it has to be an accurate knowledge, of Him that has called us to glory and virtue. God has also given us exceeding great and precious promises, not just great and precious, but *exceeding great and precious promises.* Why? That we may be partakers of His divine nature so that we can escape the corruption that is in the world through lust. We have an out even while we live here. We can apply these principals of rightly dividing the Word of God to live here victoriously.

So as you read you Bible ask yourself. Is this information that I need to know? Is this an instruction I can apply in my life and if I do what will be the beneficial result that I will gain? We can now look at some other keys to understanding the Bible.

DEAN J. SANDELL

CHAPTER 9

Orientalism, Figures Of Speech, Difficult Verses and Punctuation

Orientalism's

ORIENTALISM'S DEPICT THINGS in a culture that are unique that culture. The Bible is an eastern book and it has reference to customs found in the east and biblical times. An Americanism might be when someone has an excited outburst and says "hotdog!!!!" We understand it to mean a person is excited about something. Were a person from the East, not knowing its meaning might think of a dog on fire. One orientalism is found in Luke 6:

> 38 Give, and it shall be given unto you; good measure, pressed down, and shaken together, and running over, shall men give into your bosom. For with the same measure that ye mete withal it shall be measured to you again.

In the Jesus times when people went to market to buy, say some grain or flour, the merchant would fill their basket with the product. He would then press it down and shake it. Once he had done this he would refill the basket to the top until it ran over. He might do this several times. What Jesus was teaching here to the eastern mind they understood. He was saying that when we give, it will be given back to us, "good measure, pressed down, and shaken together, and running over, shall men give into your bosom. We will receive a full measure back from our giving. Another insight into their culture is found in Isaiah 40:

> 2 Speak ye comfortably to Jerusalem, and cry unto her, that her warfare is accomplished, that her iniquity is pardoned: for she hath received of the LORD'S hand double for all her sins.

There seems to be a contradiction here. At one point it says that her iniquity is pardoned and then it says that she hath received of the LORD'S hand double for all her sins. Whenever there seems to be a contradiction, and I emphasis the Word "seems," because the Word of God cannot contradict itself, the contradiction is either do to wrong interpretation or in our understanding. Here it would be in our understanding, because we don't understand the culture of the time.

In the eastern culture there was a place in the city where people could "post" things. One of the things posted might be a debt owed by someone to someone. If the debt was paid off or a benefactor came along and paid the debt off, the post would be doubled, hiding the debt thus showing that the debt was no longer owed. We have such a benefactor in Jesus as is recorded in

Colossians 2:

> 13 And you, being dead in your sins and the uncircumcision of your flesh, hath he quickened together with him, having forgiven you all trespasses;

> 14 Blotting out the handwriting of ordinances that was against us, which was contrary to us, and took it out of the way, nailing it to his cross;

Jesus' sacrifice for us blotted out the handwriting of ordinances that was against us, which was contrary to us, and took it out of the way, nailing it to his cross. Jesus is our benefactor and our debt was "doubled" or paid for by him.

Figures of Speech

Figures of speech used in the Bible are God's way of emphasizing or enhancing a statement. If I were to say, "the ground is dry" it would give you one sort of mental picture. But if I were to say, "the ground is thirsty" it would give you another mental picture of maybe the ground being cracked. There are many, many figures of speech used in the Bible. E.W Bullinger the great Bible scholar wrote a book called, "Figures of Speech Used in the Bible". It is a very comprehensive study of figures of speech which is not the scope of this book. But I want to look at a couple so you can get the idea of how a figure of speech is used. Ephesians 3:

17 That Christ may dwell in your hearts by faith; that ye, being rooted and grounded in love,

18 May be able to comprehend with all saints what is the breadth, and length, and depth, and height;

Notice the words, "the breadth, and length, and depth, and height". You will notice before the words, length, depth, height, the word "and" is used. This is the figure of speech "polysyndeton" or "many ands". It used to give emphasis to each word and call our attention to it.

Another figure of speech is, "hendiadys", which means, two things said one thing meant. John 4:

24 God is a Spirit: and they that worship him must worship him in spirit and in truth.

The two things said are, "spirit and in truth" the emphasis means, "spiritually truthfully" or "truly spiritually" Jesus made a statement in John 6:

63 It is the spirit that quickeneth; the flesh profiteth nothing: the words that I speak unto you, they are spirit, and they are life.

They are spirit and they are life. Literally, spiritual life.

Another figure of speech is "anthropopathei" or "condescension". This is used when human characteristics are given to God. Remember when we looked at John 4:24 where is says that "God is spirit". God does not have a form like a human. So when human characteristics are given to God it is this figure of speech. Isaiah 51:

9 Awake, awake, put on strength, O arm of the LORD; awake, as in the ancient days, in the generations of old. Art thou not it that hath cut Rahab, and wounded the dragon?

Here God is attributed with an arm. In this verse God is attributed with having a hand. Deuteronomy 2:

15 For indeed the hand of the LORD was against them, to destroy them from among the host, until they were consumed.

This gives us a metal picture of God performing something for his people against their enemies. Isaiah 59:

1 Behold, the LORD'S hand is not shortened, that it cannot save; neither his ear heavy that it cannot hear:

Here God is attributed as having a hand and an ear. This is telling us that we are never so far away from God that He can't save us, or so deaf that He can't hear us. God is sometimes attributed with having animal characteristics such as we see in Hosea 11:

> 10 They shall walk after the LORD: he shall roar like a lion: when he shall roar, then the children shall tremble from the west.

This attribute is also given, to the adversary, in 1 Peter 5:

> 8 Be sober, be vigilant; because your adversary the devil, as a roaring lion, walketh about, seeking whom he may devour:

This is giving us some insight as to the character of the adversary.

By studying the Word with an understanding of figures of speech it will give us a better understanding of the Word.

Difficult Verses

When there are a number of verses that are very clear on a subject and only a few unclear verses regarding a subject the principal that must be applied is, *the unclear verse must fit with the clear verse.* The unclear verses must not be magnified at the expense of the clear verses. When there is a predominance of clear verses, the unclear have to be studied until they fit with the clear. This is seen clearly in the subject of the dead. Although the subject of death is a very sensitive subject, we will see that the Word of God is very clear on it. It is a common acceptance that when a person dies he goes immediately to heaven. This can be very cruel when at the funeral of a child the minister tries to comfort a family by saying, "well God has another rose petal in heaven". Why on earth would God need another rose petal, and get it by taking someone's child? Here is what God says about death. Psalms 116:

15 Precious in the sight of the LORD is the death of his saints.

The usage of the word precious here might indicate that it is of some value to God when one of His saints dies. That couldn't be further from the truth. A synonym for the word precious is "costly". This would be a more accurate definition of what the death of a saint is to God. It is costly to God when one of His saints dies because what good are you to God if you are dead. Let's look another scripture that gives us great insight about death. Hebrews 2:

14 Forasmuch then as the children are partakers of flesh and blood, he also himself likewise took part of the same; that through death he might destroy him that had [or holding] the power of death, that is, the devil.

Can it be any clearer as to who the author of death is? God is light and in Him is no darkness at all. Death is certainly in the category of darkness. Let's look at some clear verses regarding the dead. Psalms 115:

17 The dead praise not the LORD, neither any that go down into silence.

Psalms 6:

4 Return, O LORD, deliver my soul: oh save me for thy mercies' sake.

5 For in death there is no remembrance of thee: in the grave who shall give thee thanks

These verses are good examples of informational verses and in the verse, interpretation verses. Here the Psalmist is asking God to deliver his soul and save him for God's mercy sake, *because* in death there is no remembrance of thee: in the grave who shall give thee thanks. It's only while we are living that we can praise God. Psalms 31:

17 Let me not be ashamed, O LORD; for I have called upon thee: let the wicked be ashamed, and let them be silent in the grave.

Ecclesiastes 9:

5 For the living know that they shall die: but the dead know not any thing, neither have they any more a reward; for the memory of them is forgotten.

6 Also their love, and their hatred, and their envy, is now perished; neither have they any more a portion for ever in any thing that is done under the sun.

Death has the same result for the wicked as it does for the saved, only the righteous will rise to incorruption but the wicked to torment. Psalms 88:

11 Shall thy lovingkindness be declared in the grave? or thy faithfulness in destruction?

So why is it so important to know that the dead are dead? It is because of the teaching of the dead being alive is a means for the adversary to deceive people. Do you remember what the first lie promulgated by the devil to Eve was? Genesis 3:

4 And the serpent said unto the woman, Ye shall not surely die.

This is the same lie being told today by well meaning people, even people in Christian circles. When a medium tells you that your dead grandmother is looking down on you or you are seeking help from the dead, you are playing right into the devils hand. If people "pray" to "saints" for help they are denying God His rightful position as God. And besides that, I'm not so sure that I want grandma knowing what I'm up to.

Let's look at this logically. If at the time of death you go straight to heaven then it would stand to reason that those who are not saved at the time of their death are immediately sent to hell for torment. They have already been judged, do they get re-judged at the judgment?

If you go straight to heaven then what is the point of the gathering together that we read about in 1 Thessalonians 4:

14 For if we believe that Jesus died and rose again, even so them also which sleep in Jesus will God bring with him.

15 For this we say unto you by the word of the Lord, that we which are alive and remain unto the coming of the Lord shall not prevent [precede] them which are asleep.

16 For the Lord himself shall descend from heaven with a shout, with the voice of the archangel, and with the trump of God: and the dead in Christ shall rise first:

If the dead are already alive, why will they have to rise first?

17 Then we which are alive and remain shall be caught up together with them in the clouds, to meet the Lord in the air: and so shall we ever be with the Lord.

18 Wherefore comfort one another with these words.

These are the words that God tells us to comfort ourselves with regarding our departed loved ones. Not that they are up there having a grand old time while we are down here fighting the devil. Why should these words comfort us? Because, they are the truth. It puts us on equal footing. God is no respecter of persons. If grandma has been dead for 100 years and has been living it up in heaven then she would have an advantage over us.

By looking at a couple of verses we can see what happens when a person dies. First in Genesis establishes when life begins. Genesis 2:

7 And the LORD God formed man of the dust of the ground, and breathed into his nostrils the breath of life; and man became a living soul.

In Genesis the account of Noah gives us some added information. Genesis 7:

13 In the selfsame day entered Noah, and Shem, and Ham, and Japheth, the sons of Noah, and Noah's wife, and the three wives of his sons with them, into the ark;

14 They, and every beast after his kind, and all the cattle after their kind, and every creeping thing that creepeth upon the earth after his kind, and every fowl after his kind, every bird of every sort.

15 And they went in unto Noah into the ark, two and two of all flesh, wherein is the breath of life.

Plants have what you would call "plant life". They don't breath in the sense that man and animals do. Fish on the other hand die if taken out of water. Let's see what happened to the inhabitants that were not in the Arc. Genesis 7:

> 21 And all flesh died that moved upon the earth, both of fowl, and of cattle, and of beast, and of every creeping thing that creepeth upon the earth, and every man:

> 22 All in whose nostrils was the breath of life, of all that was in the dry land, died.

We obviously know that without breath a person is dead. A verse in Leviticus gives us more information about life. Leviticus 17:

> 11 For the life of the flesh is in the blood: and I have given it to you upon the altar to make an atonement for your souls: for it is the blood that maketh an atonement for the soul.

Whatever keeps us alive is in the blood. This combined with breath life makes a person a living soul. There was no death in the blood of Adam and Eve. However, when they disobeyed God and turned the rulership of the earth over to Satan death entered for all mankind. I Corinthians 15:

> 26 The last enemy that shall be destroyed is death.

Jesus conquered death by his sacrifice and resurrection. His redemptive work is available to everyone who believes on him. For those who do, they will wait for his return upon death. For those who don't they will wait for the resurrection of either just or the unjust.

When a person dies, his consciousness of time ceases. However, their next conscious thought will be that of either the gathering together for believers or of judgment. That is why the Bible refers to it as sleep. When you go to sleep and wake up your next conscious thought is of you wakening.

Anyone who claims to have been taken to heaven and met with their loved ones, or tells of some experience that they had in a near death experience is not telling the truth. And what they will do to prove their point is to find a few verses that "might" imply that the dead are alive at the expense of the clear verses on the subject.

Understanding that the dead are dead does not diminish our remembrance of them or what they meant to us. It simply puts it in the right perspective of God's Word and then we won't be tricked by the adversary.

There are other subjects that this principal can apply to. Remember that we stand approved before God by rightly dividing the Word, not going along with tradition and culture. Timothy 2:

> 15 Study to shew thyself approved unto God, a workman that needeth not to be ashamed, rightly dividing the word of truth.

It is *only* by rightly dividing the Word that we stand approved.

Punctuation and Chapter Divisions

In the King James Version we need to know some things about it. First wherever you see an *italicized* word, it is an indication to us that it was added by the translators and was not in the original text that the King James was taken from. Chapter headings were put in around the 13th century and the dividing into verses occurred in the 16th century. There were no commas or any kind of punctuation in the originals. I have read that the 1611 version of the King James Bible is likely when punctuation was added. Therefore we cannot rely on chapter and verse headings and punctuation when rightly dividing the Word. But thankfully the chapter and verse headings are there to give us easy reference in finding a scripture.

Let's look a couple of chapter division errors in the Bible. John 8:

1 Jesus went unto the mount of Olives.

Now this seems simple and plan enough until you look at the context and the preceding verses of John 7:

51 Doth our law judge any man, before it hear him, and know what he doeth?

52 They answered and said unto him, Art thou also of Galilee? Search, and look: for out of Galilee ariseth no prophet.

53 And every man went unto his own house.

This is the tail end of a discourse between the people the Pharisees' and Nicodemus. Now look again at John 8:

1 Jesus went unto the mount of Olives.

It is clear that this verse should have been verse 54 of John 7, to complete the events, but the translators placed it as verse 1 of chapter 8. Let's look at 1 Corinthians 10:

31 Whether therefore ye eat, or drink, or whatsoever ye do, do all to the glory of God

32 Give none offence, neither to the Jews, nor to the Gentiles, nor to the church of God:

33 Even as I please all men in all things, not seeking mine own profit, but the profit of many, that they may be saved.

I Corinthians 11:1 Be ye followers of me, even as I also am of Christ.

Verse 1 of chapter 11 should be verse 34 of chapter 10 because verse 2 of chapter 11 starts a new thought. I Corinthians 11:

2 Now I praise you, brethren, that ye remember me in all things, and keep the ordinances, as I delivered them to you.

Let's look at one more. Philippians 3:

20 For our conversation is in heaven; from whence also we look for the Saviour, the Lord Jesus Christ:

21 Who shall change our vile body, that it may be fashioned like unto his glorious body, according to the working whereby he is able even to subdue all things unto himself.

Philippians 4:1 Therefore, my brethren dearly beloved and longed for, my joy and crown, so stand fast in the Lord, my dearly beloved.

We see here that verse 1 of chapter 4 finished the thought line of chapter 3:20&21. Looking at verse 2 of chapter 4 we see a new subject being started. Philippians 4:

2 I beseech Euodias, and beseech Syntyche, that they be of the same mind in the Lord.

3 And I intreat thee also, true yokefellow, help those women which laboured with me in the gospel, with Clement also, and with other my fellowlabourers, whose names are in the book of life.

Punctuation, particularly the use of a comma can throw a wrench in things and give a completely different perspective on words Jesus spoke. We have already seen this verse in our study of scripture build up, but I want to look at it to rightly divide what was actually said. Remember the one malefactor who didn't rail on Jesus and what Jesus said to him? We find this verse in Luke 23:

43 And Jesus said unto him, Verily I say unto thee, To day shalt thou be with me in paradise

It would appear from reading this that, Jesus was telling him that "this very day" he would be with Jesus in paradise. But could that happen? Jesus didn't go to paradise and he also said, "paradise" and not "heaven." If you remember Jesus was buried and three days later was resurrected and walked on the earth for 40 days before he ascended into "heaven". So how do we resolve this apparent contradiction? By, placing the comma, in its proper position. It should be placed after the word "today". It would then read, "verily I say unto thee today, shalt thou be with me in paradise". Jesus could make this promise of a future event because he knew that in the future there will be a paradise.

Some times in reading the Word we can clear up contradictions and misplacement of verses to give us a better understanding. We can now look at the reason that in the Old Testament there is what appears to be evil attributed to God.

CHAPTER 10

The Idiom of Permission

THERE ARE TIMES that there a apparent contradictions, and I emphasize *apparent*, because the true Word of God cannot contradict itself. One of the areas that this happens is in the matter of attributing to God evil actions. We have learned that God is light and in Him is no darkness at all. We also have learned that God is love. So how can a God of light and love cause evil on mankind? The answer is obviously a resounding, He can't. This can be explained by understanding the figure of speech, idiom of permission.

An idiom is a usage of words in a culture that have a meaning other than their strict dictionary definitions. In Figures of Speech Used in the Bible, E. W. Bullinger explained that the Hebrew language has an idiom of permission, which is a unique usage of words where active verbs are sometimes used "to express, not the doing of the thing, but the permission of the thing which the agent is said to do."

In the Old Testament times people were somewhat aware of, but not completely aware of the adversary. Part of Jesus' mission on earth was to expose the adversary. We've seen this in John 10:10 where Jesus describes the adversaries primary role is to, steal, kill and destroy. Job was aware that he had an adversary when he said in Job 31:

35 Oh that one would hear me behold, my desire is, that the Almighty would answer me, and that mine adversary had written a book.

There are other occurrences of people knowing the affects of devil spirits on a human. Jesus was confronted with one such situation in Mark 9:

18 And wheresoever he taketh him, he teareth him: and he foameth, and gnasheth with his teeth, and pineth away: and I spake to thy disciples that they should cast him out; and they could not.

19 He answereth him, and saith, O faithless generation, how long shall I be with you? how long shall I suffer you? bring him unto me.

20 And they brought him unto him: and when he saw him, straightway the spirit tare him; and he fell on the ground, and wallowed foaming.

21 And he asked his father, How long is it ago since this came unto him? And he said, Of a child.

22 And ofttimes it hath cast him into the fire, and into the waters, to destroy him: but if thou canst do any thing, have compassion on us, and help us.

23 Jesus said unto him, If thou canst believe, all things are possible to him that believeth.

24 And straightway the father of the child cried out, and said with tears, Lord, I believe; help thou mine unbelief.

DEAN J. SANDELL

25 When Jesus saw that the people came running together, he
rebuked the foul spirit, saying unto him, Thou dumb and
deaf spirit, I charge thee, come out of him, and enter no
more into him.

26 And the spirit cried, and rent him sore, and came out of
him: and he was as one dead; insomuch that many said, He
is dead.

27 But Jesus took him by the hand, and lifted him up; and he
arose.

This man came to Jesus asking for help to get his son deliverance
from the adversary. Jesus' spoke to the devil spirit and charged him
to come out and, enter no more into him. The spirits response to
Jesus was obedience after putting on a little show.

There are verses that show that God didn't even want the names of
other God's mentioned. Exodus 23:

13 And in all things that I have said unto you be circumspect:
and make no mention of the name of other gods, neither let
it be heard out of thy mouth.

Joshua 23:

7 That ye come not among these nations, these that remain
among you; neither make mention of the name of their gods,
nor cause to swear by them, neither serve them, nor bow
yourselves unto them:

God had instructed Israel not to even mention the names of other god's so that they would know that it was God who gave them victories. Joshua 23:

> 8 But cleave unto the LORD your God, as ye have done unto this day.

> 9 For the LORD hath driven out from before you great nations and strong: but as for you, no man hath been able to stand before you unto this day.

> 10 One man of you shall chase a thousand: for the LORD your God, he it is that fighteth for you, as he hath promised you.

> 11 Take good heed therefore unto yourselves, that ye love the LORD your God.

Because of their limited knowledge of the spirit realm, and because God wanted them to keep their focus on Him, they would attribute evil happenings to God.

One other thing we must consider is man's free will. God will never overstep a person's ability to choose, even if it is going to be harmful to the person. That is because God is love and will not overstep the person's free will. This is evident even in the fall of Lucifer. God could not stop Lucifer from making the idiotic decision to rebel against God. Deuteronomy 11:

> 26 Behold, I set before you this day a blessing and a curse;

> 27 A blessing, if ye obey the commandments of the LORD your God, which I command you this day:

28 And a curse, if ye will not obey the commandments of the LORD your God, but turn aside out of the way which I command you this day, to go after other gods, which ye have not known.

The choice is clear. A blessing if you choose God and a curse if you choose the other god, i.e. the adversary. Joshua 24:

15 And if it seem evil unto you to serve the LORD, choose you this day whom ye will serve; whether the gods which your fathers served that were on the other side of the flood, or the gods of the Amorites, in whose land ye dwell: but as for me and my house, we will serve the LORD.

It is clear that serving any other god's, which are no gods but a front for the adversary, will bring dire results. So let's look at some incidences of the usage of the figure of speech, idiom of permission. 2 Samuel 24:

1 And again the anger of the LORD was kindled against Israel, and he [the Lord] moved [permitted David to be moved] against them to say, Go, number Israel and Judah.

II Samuel is written from man's point of view, while the book of Chronicles is written from God's point of view and reveals what really was going on. 1 Chronicles 21:

1 And Satan stood up against Israel, and provoked David to number Israel.

So we can see from this, who was really influencing David and because of his free will God had to allow David to number Israel. In I Chronicles' we see the death of Saul during a battle. I Chronicles 10:

3 And the battle went sore against Saul, and the archers hit him, and he was wounded of the archers.

4 Then said Saul to his armourbearer, Draw thy sword, and thrust me through therewith; lest these uncircumcised come and abuse me. But his armourbearer would not; for he was sore afraid. So Saul took a sword, and fell upon it.

5 And when his armourbearer saw that Saul was dead, he fell likewise on the sword, and died.

It appears here that Saul killed himself. Which he did. But, we will see by reading a little further, what was the cause behind it. I Chronicles 10:

13 So Saul died for his transgression which he committed against the LORD, even against the word of the LORD, which he kept not, and also for asking counsel of one that had a familiar spirit, to enquire of it;

14 And enquired not of the LORD: therefore he [the Lord] slew him,[allowed Saul to be slain] and turned the kingdom unto David the son of Jesse.

Saul had transgressed against God by asking counsel of one that had a familiar spirit, [a medium, one who supposedly can contact the dead which is actually contacting a devil spirit] to enquire of it, which was against the Word of the Lord. Saul chose to not enquire of God for the thing that concerned him and this opened him up to be killed.

Now let's look at the smiting of the first born Eqyptians. Exodus 12:

29 And it came to pass, that at midnight the LORD [permitted to be] smote all the firstborn in the land of Egypt, from the firstborn of Pharaoh that sat on his throne unto the firstborn of the captive that was in the dungeon; and all the firstborn of cattle.

If you read Exodus you will see that Moses pleaded with Pharaoh to let God's people go. They had even suffered plagues, the Nile turning to blood, frogs and all shots of things to go on before this event occurred. The idiom is used of what Pharaoh allowed to happen to his heart. Exodus 7:

13 And he [the Lord] hardened Pharaoh's heart, that he hearkened not unto them; as the LORD had said.

14 And the LORD said unto Moses, Pharaoh's heart is hardened, he refuseth to let the people go.

It again appears that God did this when we can see that it was Pharaoh who hardened his heart by refusing to let the people go. We can see this in Exodus 8:

15 But when Pharaoh saw that there was respite, he hardened his heart, and hearkened not unto them; as the LORD had said.

So we see here that it was a matter of choice on Pharaoh's part. Now back to the slaying of the first born. Exodus 12:

21 Then Moses called for all the elders of Israel, and said unto them, Draw out and take you a lamb according to your families, and kill the passover.

22 And ye shall take a bunch of hyssop, and dip it in the blood that is in the bason, and strike the lintel and the two side

posts with the blood that is in the bason; and none of you shall go out at the door of his house until the morning.

God had given specific instruction to the Israelites on how to protect themselves. If any Egyptians would have done the same thing their children would be spared as well. We will now see in the next verse what really happened.

23 For the LORD will pass through to [permit the smiting of] the Egyptians; and when he seeth the blood upon the lintel, and on the two side posts, the LORD will pass over the door, and will not suffer [permit] the destroyer [the Devil] to come in unto your houses to smite you.

God will always give us the protection we need against the Devil as long as we will obey His Word. The figure of speech, idiom of permission, opens our eyes to what really caused the different events recorded in the Old Testament. Things like the flood, Sodom and Gomorrah as well as many others.

What about the administration of Grace that we live in? The only reference of this figure that I can think of is found in II Thessalonians and it is in the context of the antichrist. II Thessalonians 2:

9 Even him, whose coming is after the working of Satan with all power and signs and lying wonders,

10 And with all deceivableness of unrighteousness in them that perish; because they received not the love of the truth, that they might be saved.

11 And for this cause God shall send them strong delusion, that they should believe a lie:

We can even see here why they will be in delusion. "Because, they received not the love of the truth, that they might be saved."

We have an advantage, because with the work of Jesus we can now see what is going on. We have seen in I Peter that we are to be sober and vigilant. 1 Peter 5:

> 8 Be sober, be vigilant; because your adversary the devil, as a roaring lion, walketh about, seeking whom he may devour:
>
> 9 Whom resist stedfast in the faith, knowing that the same afflictions are accomplished in your brethren that are in the world.
>
> 10 But the God of all grace, who hath called us unto his eternal glory by Christ Jesus, after that ye have suffered a while, make you perfect, stablish, strengthen, settle you.
>
> 11 To him be glory and dominion for ever and ever. Amen.

It is the God of all grace that makes you perfect, established, strengthens, settles us, as we resist steadfast in the family faith and remember were not in this alone. Our fellow believers are also having to deal with defeating the devil. God gives us an instruction on dealing with the adversary in James 4:

> 7 Submit yourselves therefore to God. Resist the devil, and he will flee from you.
>
> 8 Draw nigh to God, and he will draw nigh to you. Cleanse your hands, ye sinners; and purify your hearts, ye double minded.

Look at what else God says in James 2:

19 Thou believest that there is one God; thou doest well: the devils also believe, and tremble.

That is some good news to have. We can make devils tremble when we stand on the Word.

In the book of Ephesians it is clearly spelled out what we are up against Ephesians 6:

10 Finally, my brethren, be strong in the Lord, and in the power of his might.

11 Put on the whole armour of God, that ye may be able to stand against the wiles of the devil.

12 For we wrestle not against flesh and blood, but against principalities, against powers, against the rulers of the darkness of this world, against spiritual wickedness in high places.

13 Wherefore take unto you the whole armour of God, that ye may be able to withstand in the evil day, and having done all, to stand.

We as believers in this administration have a huge advantage over the believers of the Old Testament. Because we are born again of God's Spirit and have Christ in us the hope of glory. 1 John 3:

8 He that committeth sin is of the devil; for the devil sinneth from the beginning. For this purpose the Son of God was manifested, that he might destroy the works of the devil.

Yes folks, there are sinners out there, they are around us but look at the reason Jesus was manifested. *That he might destroy the works of the devil*. That is our purpose also. We are to destroy the works of the devil that he may be using to afflict us, cause poverty or steal away any of the promises that God has given us. And on top of that, God has equipped us with holy spirit and the manifestations of the spirit to engage and win. 1 Corinthians 12:

> 7 But the manifestation of the Spirit is given to every man to profit withal.

> 8 For to one is given by the Spirit the word of wisdom; to another the word of knowledge by the same Spirit;

> 9 To another faith by the same Spirit; to another the gifts of healing by the same Spirit;

> 10 To another the working of miracles; to another prophecy; to another discerning of spirits; to another divers kinds of tongues; to another the interpretation of tongues:

> 11 But all these worketh that one and the selfsame Spirit, dividing to every man severally as he [the man] will.

These nine manifestations are our weapons in this warfare. We have discerning of spirits, word of wisdom, word of knowledge, working of miracles and gifts of healing, as a means to deal with and destroy the works of the adversary. These are the same manifestations that Jesus used in his ministry to heal and deliver people. Except speaking in tongues because that was not available until the day of Pentecost.

With the study of the figure of speech, idiom of permission, we now know that God is a good God always and that the evil in the world is of the devil. When an insurance company says they will not cover certain "acts of god" we know that they are talking about the god of this world and not our father and God. We can no longer be tricked into thinking that the bad things of the world are of the true God.

With all that we have learned we can now look at a principal in the Word that will give us the power of the Word of God in our lives. And that principal is ….

CHAPTER 11

The Renewed Mind

The principal of the renewed mind is found in Romans 12:

1 I beseech you therefore, brethren, by the mercies of God, that ye present your bodies a living sacrifice, holy, acceptable unto God, which is your reasonable service.

2 And be not conformed to this world: but be ye transformed by the renewing of your mind, that ye may prove what is that good, and acceptable, and perfect, will of God.

3 For I say, through the grace given unto me, to every man that is among you, not to think of himself more highly than he ought to think; but to think soberly, according as God hath dealt to every man the measure of faith.

WITHOUT THE RENEWED mind we will never experience the good, acceptable and perfect will of God in our lives. God admonishes us to think soberly (soundly) "according as God hath dealt to every man the measure of faith." That measure of faith is the faith of Jesus Christ that we received when we were born again. Every person born again, receives the same amount.

Why is it necessary for us as children of God to renew our minds? Ephesians 2:

1 And you hath he quickened [made alive], who were dead in trespasses and sins;

2 Wherein in time past ye walked according to the course of this world, according to the prince of the power of the air, the spirit that now worketh in the children of disobedience:

3 Among whom also we all had our conversation in times past in the lusts of our flesh, fulfilling the desires of the flesh and of the mind; and were by nature the children of wrath, even as others.

When we were born, we were, as verse 12 tells us,

12 That at that time ye were without Christ, being aliens from the commonwealth of Israel, and strangers from the covenants of promise, having no hope, and without God in the world:

All people are born without God, holy spirit. As we grew up we, "walked according to the course of this world, according to the prince of the power of the air, the spirit that now worketh in the children of disobedience. And we also, "all had our conversation in times past in the lusts of our flesh, fulfilling the desires of the flesh and of the mind; and were by nature the children of wrath, even as others." We were simply a body and soul person. But God quickened [made alive] us while, we were dead in trespasses and sins. But look at what God did.

Ephesians 2:

4 But God, who is rich in mercy, for his great love wherewith he loved us,

DEAN J. SANDELL

5 Even when we were dead in sins, hath quickened [made alive] us together with Christ, (by grace ye are saved;)

6 And hath raised us up together, and made us sit together in heavenly places in Christ Jesus:

7 That in the ages to come he might shew the exceeding riches of his grace in his kindness toward us through Christ Jesus.

8 For by grace are ye saved through faith; and that not of yourselves: it is the gift of God:

Now that is a loving God. He made us alive with Christ Jesus. And note, "by grace ye are saved through faith; and that not of yourselves: it is the gift of God". Remember the administration we are living in? Grace. Verse 7 gives us the reason for Him doing this. *That in the ages to come he might shew the exceeding riches of his grace in his kindness toward us through Christ Jesus.* Remember the types of verses we looked at? These verses are giving us some vital information. Ephesians 2:

10 For we are his workmanship, created in Christ Jesus unto good works, which God hath before ordained that we should walk in them.

11 Wherefore remember, that ye being in time past Gentiles in the flesh, who are called Uncircumcision by that which is called the Circumcision in the flesh made by hands;

12 That at that time ye were without Christ, being aliens from the commonwealth of Israel, and strangers from the covenants of promise, having no hope, and without God in the world:

13 But now in Christ Jesus ye who sometimes were far off are made nigh by the blood of Christ.

14 For he is our peace, who hath made both one, and hath broken down the middle wall of partition between us;

We are God's workmanship. This happened when we were born again and we were "created", receiving holy spirit, unto good works. These good works we are to "walk" in. In order to do that we have to renew, change up, our minds from walking after the course of this world, to walking according to the Word. This can only be done by the putting on of the Word in our minds and learning to not walk *according to the course of this world, according to the prince of the power of the air,* but to walk according to the Word.

Walking according to the Word is an action that we take by our freedom of will. There are several scriptures that instruct us about walking. Romans 6:

4 Therefore we are buried with him by baptism into death: that like as Christ was raised up from the dead by the glory of the Father, even so we also should walk in newness of life.

We now have the holy spirit, Christ in us, and because of this we can walk in this newness of life. Look at what Romans has to say about this. Romans 8:

1 There is therefore now no condemnation to them which are in Christ Jesus, who walk not after the flesh, but after the Spirit.

2 For the law of the Spirit of life in Christ Jesus hath made me free from the law of sin and death.

3 For what the law could not do, in that it was weak through the flesh, God sending his own Son in the likeness of sinful flesh, and for sin, condemned sin in the flesh:

4 That the righteousness of the law might be fulfilled in us, who walk not after the flesh, but after the Spirit.

5 For they that are after the flesh do mind the things of the flesh; but they that are after the Spirit the things of the Spirit.

6 For to be carnally minded is death; but to be spiritually minded is life and peace.

7 Because the carnal mind is enmity against God: for it is not subject to the law of God, neither indeed can be.

8 So then they that are in the flesh cannot please God.

God does not want us walking by our senses because God wants us to walk by the Spirit He has placed in us. We do this by studying the Word and then putting it on in our minds. To be carnal (senses orientated) in our thinking is enmity (at odds with) God.

Before we begin our study of how to renew our mind and learn to walk in the spirit, I want to look at the word mind.

Different Minds Found In The Bible

One of the Greek word for mind is the word *nous* (pronounced noose) and it refers to the organ of mental perception. The *nous* is fed and influenced by either the five senses or a spirit whether it be holy spirit or a devil spirit. It receives information and collects data and through reasoning makes decisions. Unlike the brain, which is a physical organ, the mind is a part of man that can't be taken out and dissected like a physical organ. However, the mind plays a most important part in our lives. That's why it is so important to understand the mind in light of God's Word. Let's look at some of the kinds of minds found in the Bible. II Corinthians 4:

> 4 In whom the god of this world hath blinded the minds of them which believe not, lest the light of the glorious gospel of Christ, who is the image of God, should shine unto them.

A blinded mind is one that, obviously can't see. This is the intent of the adversary to not let people see *the light of the glorious gospel of Christ, who is the image of God*. He does this through peoples five sense using lies and deception. 2 Corinthians 11:

> 13 For such are false apostles, deceitful workers, transforming themselves into the apostles of Christ.

> 14 And no marvel; for Satan himself is transformed into an angel of light.

> 15 Therefore it is no great thing if his ministers also be transformed as the ministers of righteousness; whose end shall be according to their works.

Ephesians 4:

> 14 That we henceforth be no more children, tossed to and fro, and carried about with every wind of doctrine, by the sleight of men, and cunning craftiness, whereby they lie in wait to deceive;

DEAN J. SANDELL

The adversaries' main attempt is to not let people get born again. However, there are also people who are born again and his mission then is to blind their minds, so that they don't see what is available to them as a believer, and blinds their minds so that they live less then what they can if they were to have the glorious gospel shine upon them. Look at what God's will is for the believer. Ephesians 1:

15 Wherefore I also, after I heard of your faith in the Lord Jesus, and love unto all the saints,

16 Cease not to give thanks for you, making mention of you in my prayers;

17 That the God of our Lord Jesus Christ, the Father of glory, may give unto you the spirit of wisdom and revelation in the knowledge of him:

18 The eyes of your understanding being enlightened; that ye may know what is the hope of his calling, and what the riches of the glory of his inheritance in the saints,

19 And what is the exceeding greatness of his power to us-ward who believe, according to the working of his mighty power,

That is God's will for you. The eyes of your understanding being *enlightened*, that you may *know* what is the hope of His calling, and the *riches* of the glory, and what is the *exceeding greatness* of His power toward us who believe. Do you see now why the adversary wants to blind people's minds? Another type of mind found in the Word is in Romans 1:

28 And even as they did not like to retain God in their knowledge, God gave them over to a reprobate mind, to do those things which are not convenient;

A reprobate mind is defined as one that is, unprincipled, morally depraved, without soundness. The reason that they developed this type of mind is because, *they did not like to retain God in their knowledge.* These people become a god unto themselves and are subject to the suggestions of the adversary and his bidding. They promote, unwittingly and maybe with malice intent, the agenda of the adversary. On the other hand look at what God has given us as found in 2 Timothy 1:

7 For God hath not given us the spirit of fear; but of power, and of love, and of a sound mind.

God has given to us the potential of a sound mind. Having whole thoughts based upon His Word. I say potential because simply being born again does not guarantee that we will have them. That is where the renewed mind comes in. Another type of mind is found in Romans 8:

5 For they that are after the flesh do mind the things of the flesh; but they that are after the Spirit the things of the Spirit.

6 For to be carnally minded is death; but to be spiritually minded is life and peace.

7 Because the carnal mind is enmity against God: for it is not subject to the law of God, neither indeed can be.

8 So then they that are in the flesh cannot please God.

A carnal mind is a mind that is governed by the five senses. We are told in verse 6 that a carnal mind is death and in verse 7 that it is enmity against God. It is not subject to the law of God. On the other side, in verse 6 we are told that to be spiritually minded is life and peace.

We can now see that man makes his decisions based on what knowledge he has obtained. There are two kinds of knowledge. There is natural knowledge and spiritual knowledge. Looking at natural knowledge we will find that it is limited. That's because it is obtained through the five senses. It is received by works and is unreliable and based on facts. While this is good and important for mankind to have it is not the same as spiritual knowledge. Spiritual knowledge is first, unlimited, because it comes from God, who can reveal things from the spiritual realm to us by His Holy Spirit. It is given by grace, God's divine favor to us. It is reliable because God is reliable and it is truth. Jesus stated in John 17:

17 Sanctify them through thy truth: thy word is truth.

And in John chapter 16 Jesus said, John 16:

13 Howbeit when he, the Spirit of truth, is come, he will guide you into all truth: for he shall not speak of himself; but whatsoever he shall hear, that shall he speak: and he will shew you things to come.

Remember that God cannot lie. However, the adversary is the father of lies. John 8:

44 Ye are of your father the devil, and the lusts of your father ye will do. He was a murderer from the beginning, and abode not in the truth, because there is no truth in him. When he

speaketh a lie, he speaketh of his own: for he is a liar, and the father of it.

So we are faced with a choice. To either believe the lies of the adversary or the truth from God. Let's look another mind. 1 Corinthians 2:

16 For who hath known the mind of the Lord, that he may instruct him? But we have the mind of Christ.

At the time of the new birth, we receive holy spirit, Christ in us. This gives us again the potential of having the mind of Christ. How do we utilize that mind? Philippians 2:

5 Let this mind be in you, which was also in Christ Jesus:

It is by our freewill choice that we can have the mind of Christ and walk as he walked.

So we have seen from the Word different kinds of minds. So where do we begin with this walk by the spirit? 2 Timothy 3:

16 All scripture is given by inspiration of God, and is profitable for doctrine, for reproof, for correction, for instruction in righteousness:

We start, by realizing the all scripture is God breathed as we have studied before. We see that it is profitable for doctrine, right believing, reproof, correcting us when we are not believing rightly and for correction to show us how to get back to right believing. This is done by what we are instructed to do in 2 Timothy 2:

15 Study to shew thyself approved unto God, a workman that needeth not to be ashamed, rightly dividing the word of truth.

We start by going to the Word and reading it so we can learn what God has done for us through Jesus Christ and what we have because of what Christ did for us. Since the Bible is the reveled Word and Will of God, the only way we will know God's will for our lives is to read it and study it. We are then instructed on how to apply it in our lives. Romans 14:

> 19 Let us therefore follow after the things which make for peace, and things wherewith one may edify another.

Whenever you see the word "let" it is telling us to make a conscious decision to do something. Let's look at some other usages of "let". Galatians 5:

> 25 If we live in the Spirit, let us also walk in the Spirit.

Here we are told to *walk in the spirit*. Colossians 3:

> 15 And let the peace of God rule in your hearts, to the which also ye are called in one body; and be ye thankful.

These are simply choices we have to decide to make. *Let the peace of God rule in your hearts* and *and be ye thankful*. This is to our benefit. Philippians 2:

> 5 Let this mind be in you, which was also in Christ Jesus.

Remember that when we received Christ Jesus we received his mind spiritually. We let his mind be in us by reading about Jesus and thinking the way he did. Another instruction to us that will benefit us is, "put on". This is another act that we do by a conscious decision of our will. Ephesians 4:

22 That ye put off concerning the former conversation the old man, which is corrupt according to the deceitful lusts;

23 And be renewed in the spirit of your mind;

24 And that ye put on the new man, which after God is created in righteousness and true holiness.

Here we are told to do two things. One is, *put off* the old man [our former nature] and to, *put on* the new man [Christ in you]. Then in verses 25- 32 we are given specific instruction on how to do this.

25 Wherefore putting away lying, speak every man truth with his neighbour: for we are members one of another.

26 Be ye angry, and sin not: let not the sun go down upon your wrath:

27 Neither give place to the devil.

28 Let him that stole steal no more: but rather let him labour, working with his hands the thing which is good, that he may have to give to him that needeth.

29 Let no corrupt communication proceed out of your mouth, but that which is good to the use of edifying, that it may minister grace unto the hearers.

30 And grieve not the holy Spirit of God, whereby ye are sealed unto the day of redemption.

31 Let all bitterness, and wrath, and anger, and clamour, and evil speaking, be put away from you, with all malice:

DEAN J. SANDELL

32 And be ye kind one to another, tenderhearted, forgiving one another, even as God for Christ's sake hath forgiven you.

Verse 30 tells us to not grieve the Holy Spirit of God. We grieve the Holy Spirit by not doing what God instructs us to do.

As we do these things we will begin to prove what is that that good, and acceptable, and perfect, will of God in our lives. Another thing we can do that will help us to renew our minds is to "think". We are always thinking why not think on the things God tells us to? Philippians 4:

8 Finally, brethren, whatsoever things are true, whatsoever things are honest, whatsoever things are just, whatsoever things are pure, whatsoever things are lovely, whatsoever things are of good report; if there be any virtue, and if there be any praise, think on these things.

9 Those things, which ye have both learned, and received, and heard, and seen in me, do: and the God of peace shall be with you

What we think about the most will manifest itself in our lives. The very famous book by Napoleon Hill, Think and Grow Rich, is a prime example of teaching people the importance of what their thinking can produce. Imagine what we can produce by controlling our thinking to be in alignment with God's Word. Proverbs 23:

6 Eat thou not the bread of him that hath an evil eye, neither desire thou his dainty meats:

7 For as he thinketh in his heart, so is he: Eat and drink, saith he to thee; but his heart is not with thee.

God is warning us of deceitful people. They will say one thing to you but inwardly they are against you because his thinking has produced an evil heart. On the other side of this is, if this is applied in a Godly sense it will produce good in our lives. Proverbs 4:

> 20 My son, attend to my words; incline thine ear unto my sayings.

> 21 Let them not depart from thine eyes; keep them in the midst of thine heart.

> 22 For they are life unto those that find them, and health to all their flesh.

> 23 Keep thy heart with all diligence; for out of it are the issues of life.

As we put Gods words into our minds and they reach our heart, the innermost part of our being from which faith or fear emanates, Gods words will produce *life unto those that find them, and health to all their flesh.* We are told to keep, or guard, are hearts, with all diligence because it determines the outcomes in our lives. How many times have we heard someone say, "boy that person really has some issues". God doesn't look at us senses wise. 1 Samuel 16:

> 7 But the LORD said unto Samuel, Look not on his countenance, or on the height of his stature; because I have refused him: for the LORD seeth not as man seeth; for man looketh on the outward appearance, but the LORD looketh on the heart.

God is able to look at the heart of a person and see the real person. We want it so that when God looks at us He sees a genuine heart which we have by believing His Word.

Before we end this study I want to cover another process of the renewed mind.

Confessing The Word Out Loud

We live in a world of words. This is the way that man communicates. We are faced each day with either words (lies) of the adversary or words (truth) from God. Hebrews 4:

> 12 For the word of God is quick, and powerful, and sharper than any twoedged sword, piercing even to the dividing asunder of soul and spirit, and of the joints and marrow, and is a discerner of the thoughts and intents of the heart.

God's words are quick [makes alive], powerful, sharper than any two edged sword. God's Word gets to the heart of things and can even give us insight into the thoughts and intents of the heart, man's inner most being, from which either good or evil derives from. The Bible has a lot to say about the tongue. One of the most referenced is found in James 3:

> 5 Even so the tongue is a little member, and boasteth great things. Behold, how great a matter a little fire kindleth!

> 6 And the tongue is a fire, a world of iniquity: so is the tongue among our members, that it defileth the whole body, and setteth on fire the course of nature; and it is set on fire of hell.

> 7 For every kind of beasts, and of birds, and of serpents, and of things in the sea, is tamed, and hath been tamed of mankind:

> 8 But the tongue can no man tame; it is an unruly evil, full of deadly poison.

9 Therewith bless we God, even the Father; and therewith curse we men, which are made after the similitude of God.

10 Out of the same mouth proceedeth blessing and cursing. My brethren, these things ought not so to be.

11 Doth a fountain send forth at the same place sweet water and bitter?

12 Can the fig tree, my brethren, bear olive berries? either a vine, figs? so can no fountain both yield salt water and fresh.

As we can see the tongue is a powerful tool. So if we can learn to confess what God says then we can have what God wants us to have. However if we confess what the adversary says, we will have what the adversary wants us to have. Luke 6:

45 A good man out of the good treasure of his heart bringeth forth that which is good; and an evil man out of the evil treasure of his heart bringeth forth that which is evil: for of the abundance of the heart his mouth speaketh.

What we think on is what gets into our hearts and then we eventually will speak it out.

If we are focus is on ill health and we speak it the result will be ill health but if we focus on what Christ accomplished for us and speak that we will have good health. 1 Peter 2:

24 Who his own self bare our sins in his own body on the tree, that we, being dead to sins, should live unto righteousness: by whose stripes ye were [are, present tense] healed.

If that is what you are confessing then God has to perform His Word and heal you. A verse in Romans makes it very clear how are beliefs are made. Romans 10:

> 17 So then faith cometh by hearing, and hearing by the word of God.

Faith, believing, comes by hearing. When you hear something you take it in, digest it, and decide to believe it or not. This works for both the adversary's words, or God's Word. How important is confessing? Romans 10:

> 9 That if thou shalt confess with thy mouth the Lord Jesus, and shalt believe in thine heart that God hath raised him from the dead, thou shalt be saved.

> 10 For with the heart man believeth unto righteousness; and with the mouth confession is made unto salvation.

Someone gave you information about Jesus. You decided in your heart to believe it. Your confession is what got you saved. The reason we make our confession and make it out loud is so that we can hear our own voice make statements to our mind. This "hearing" is what will build our faith and believing and eventually bring to pass our desired results. This same principal is what gets us answered prayer. Jesus taught this principal to his disciples. Mark 11:

> 12 And on the morrow, when they were come from Bethany, he was hungry:

> 13 And seeing a fig tree afar off having leaves, he came, if haply he might find any thing thereon: and when he came to it, he found nothing but leaves; for the time of figs was not yet.

14 And Jesus answered and said unto it, No man eat fruit of thee hereafter for ever. And his disciples heard it.

What did Jesus' disciples hear? Jesus, talking to a tree. He cursed it. What do you think he expected to happen to it? We'll see what happened. Mark 11:

19 And when even was come, he went out of the city.

20 And in the morning, as they passed by, they saw the fig tree dried up from the roots.

21 And Peter calling to remembrance saith unto him, Master, behold, the fig tree which thou cursedst is withered away.

This sure got Peters attention. However, it was certainly no surprise to Jesus because, he knew the power of the spoken word. He was simply following the example set by his father.

Remember the account of God putting the earth back together in Genesis? What did God do?

If you read the account you will see that, "and God said", and the end result was, "it was so. Jesus responded to Peter's observation. Mark 11:

22 And Jesus answering saith unto them, Have faith in God.

23 For verily I say unto you, That whosoever shall say unto this mountain, Be thou removed, and be thou cast into the sea; and shall not doubt in his heart, but shall believe that those things which he saith shall come to pass; he shall have whatsoever he saith.

24 Therefore I say unto you, What things soever ye desire, when ye pray, believe that ye receive them, and ye shall have them.

First Jesus instructs them to "have faith in God". Then he gives them the how. He states, "whosoever shall say", "believe those things which he saith", "he shall [absolutely] have whatsoever he saith". Also note that Jesus didn't "think" unto the fig tree he "spoke" to it.

The apostles asked of Jesus a request. Luke 17:

5 And the apostles said unto the Lord, Increase our faith.

6 And the Lord said, If ye had faith as a grain of mustard seed, ye might say unto this sycamine tree, Be thou plucked up by the root, and be thou planted in the sea; and it should obey you.

That's a pretty good request. His instruction to them again was, "say". To increase your faith, it is necessary to speak. The more you hear yourself speak words of faith, it will increase. We can imitate God by operating like God. Romans 4:

17 (As it is written, I have made thee a father of many nations,) before him whom he believed, even God, who quickeneth the dead, and calleth those things which be not as though they were.

This is how God operates. Jesus operated this way in his ministry. He told leopards to go show themselves to the priest before they were healed, and they received their healing on the way. He told a blind man to go wash in the pool of Siloam before he was healed, and he got healed. Hebrews 10:

23 Let us hold fast the profession [confession] of our faith without wavering; (for he is faithful that promised;)

God is faithful to perform His Word if, we will be faithful to keep confessing it until we receive it.

I think this principal is not used by Christians because, they don't realize the power of words, whether they be the words of the adversary or the words of God.

We live in a world of words. Every day there is a battle going on for the minds and hearts of mankind. This started in the Garden of Eden, "hath God really said", was the question.

Each day we are inundated with words from the media, friends, coworkers, or even overhearing a stranger's conversation. It is up to us to weigh these words in light of God's Word. The economy, health (commercials for medicine where the side effects are worse than the disease), race and sex relations.

I am writing this just a couple of days before the presidential election of 2016. The war of words between these two candidates has been like nothing before. So how do I balance what is being said on TV and God. Let's look at a couple of verses. Philippians 2:

13 For it is God which worketh in you both to will and to do of his good pleasure.

14 Do all things without murmurings and disputings:

15 That ye may be blameless and harmless, the sons of God, without rebuke, in the midst of a crooked and perverse nation, among whom ye shine as lights in the world;

God is fully aware of the condition of the world, but tells us that we can shine as lights in the world. This can only be if we put on the word. Galatians 1:

3 Grace be to you and peace from God the Father, and from our Lord Jesus Christ,

4 Who gave himself for our sins, that he might deliver us from this present evil world, according to the will of God and our Father:

We can be delivered from this present evil world while we are still living in it because, of the Christ in us, if we will deliberately put on the mind of Christ. Colossians 1:

13 Who hath delivered us from the power of darkness, and hath translated us into the kingdom of his dear Son:

It is by what Christ accomplished that we are in God's kingdom. 2 Peter 1:

2 Grace and peace be multiplied unto you through the knowledge of God, and of Jesus our Lord,

3 According as his divine power hath given unto us all things that pertain unto life and godliness, through the knowledge of him that hath called us to glory and virtue:

4 Whereby are given unto us exceeding great and precious promises: that by these ye might be partakers of the divine nature, having escaped the corruption that is in the world through lust.

It is only through a knowledge of him that we receive great and precious promises. When we learn and apply these great and precious promises, we partake of the divine nature and escape the corruption that is in this world through lust [over desire]. Ephesians 2:

> 6 And hath raised us up together, and made us sit together in heavenly places in Christ Jesus:

While we are still living in this corrupt world, we are also seated in the heavenlies by Christ accomplishments. We just have to learn to appropriate those promises. 1 John 4:

> 4 Ye are of God, little children, and have overcome them: because greater is he that is in you, than he that is in the world.

> 5 They are of the world: therefore speak they of the world, and the world heareth them.

> 6 We are of God: he that knoweth God heareth us; he that is not of God heareth not us. Hereby know we the spirit of truth, and the spirit of error.

Can you bring yourself to believe that greater is he that is in us than he who is in the world? Who is in the world? The adversary. Who is in us? Christ. People in the world, those governed by their five senses, hear the world. We are of God, and by learning about God, we can hear Him. This gives us a unique advantage that we can know both the spirit of true and the spirit of error.

We must renew are minds to see God at work in our lives then we must operate as God does. Once we start this process, a lifelong one by the way, we must then learn to walk as God would have us walk. God gives us an instruction on this in Ephesians 4

DEAN J. SANDELL

17 This I say therefore, and testify in the Lord, that ye henceforth walk not as other Gentiles walk, in the vanity [perverseness, depravity] of their mind,

Because of the availability of a sound mind when we renew it to the word we don't have to walk as unbelievers. Galatians 5:

16 This I say then, Walk in the Spirit, and ye shall not fulfil the lust of the flesh.

We as believers have a choice. Ephesians 2:

10 For we are his workmanship, created in Christ Jesus unto good works, which God hath before ordained that we should walk in them.

Ephesians 4:

1 I therefore, the prisoner of the Lord, beseech you that ye walk worthy of the vocation wherewith ye are called,

We are called of God unto good works, such as faith, integrity, health, wisdom just to mention a few. The best walk we can walk in is love. Ephesians 5:

2 And walk in love, as Christ also hath loved us, and hath given himself for us an offering and a sacrifice to God for a sweet smelling savour.

When we walk in love we are fulfilling the calling upon our lives as sons of God. This will protect us from the world around us and keep us living victoriously. But we can only accomplish this by the renewing of our minds.

CHAPTER 12

Born Again Of Incorruptible Seed

1 PETER 1:23 BEING born again, not of corruptible seed, but of incorruptible, by the word of God, which liveth and abideth for ever.

What is it to be born again? The term is very common and known to almost everyone. Let's look at a verse in John 3:

> 1 There was a man of the Pharisees, named Nicodemus, a ruler of the Jews:
>
> 2 The same came to Jesus by night, and said unto him, Rabbi, we know that thou art a teacher come from God: for no man can do these miracles that thou doest, except God be with him.
>
> 3 Jesus answered and said unto him, Verily, verily, I say unto thee, Except a man be born again, he cannot see the kingdom of God.
>
> 4 Nicodemus saith unto him, How can a man be born when he is old? can he enter the second time into his mother's womb, and be born?

5 Jesus answered, Verily, verily, I say unto thee, Except a man be born of water and of the Spirit, he cannot enter into the kingdom of God.

6 That which is born of the flesh is flesh; and that which is born of the Spirit is spirit.

7 Marvel not that I said unto thee, Ye must be born again.

This Nicodemus, as we can see was a Pharisees, religious leader and a ruler of the Jews. Notice that he came to Jesus by night. He knew that if he were seen with Jesus it could jeopardize his position in the community. However, he recognized something about Jesus that he made clear when he said to Jesus, "Rabbi, we know that thou art a teacher come from God: for no man can do these miracles that thou doest, except God be with him." The conversation continues as Jesus say's to him, "Verily, verily, I say unto thee, except a man be born again, he cannot see the kingdom of God." This is a very profound statement for Nicodemus and asks a legitimate question. "How can a man be born when he is old? Can he enter the second time into his mother's womb, and be born?" Jesus then says unto him, "Verily, verily, I say unto thee, except a man be born of water and of the Spirit, he cannot enter into the kingdom of God.

That which is born of the flesh is flesh; and that which is born of the Spirit is spirit. Marvel not that I said unto thee, ye must be born again."

Jesus is actually telling him of future events because it was not yet available to be born again at that time. Jesus references two different types of birth when he says, "except a man be born of water and of the Spirit". Reference to being born of water is referring to the natural birth of all human beings. When the "water" brakes in a woman's womb the process of birth begins and the end result it a baby. That is what Jesus was saying about being born of the flesh. We are all born of the flesh but being born of the Spirit is a different act involving God. Up until the time to the new birth man is simply body and soul also called a natural man. I Corinthians 2:

> 12 Now we have received, not the spirit of the world, but the spirit which is of God; that we might know the things that are freely given to us of God.

> 13 Which things also we speak, not in the words which man's wisdom teacheth, but which the Holy Ghost teacheth; comparing spiritual things with spiritual.

> 14 But the natural man receiveth not the things of the Spirit of God: for they are foolishness unto him: neither can he know them, because they are spiritually discerned.

> 15 But he that is spiritual judgeth all things, yet he himself is judged of no man.

> 16 For who hath known the mind of the Lord, that he may instruct him? But we have the mind of Christ.

We know from verse 2 of the first chapter of Corinthians to whom Paul was writing, born again believers. Here in verse 12 he tells us that we have received the spirit from God so that we might know the things *freely given* to us by God. He tells us in verse 13 that he was not teaching them man's wisdom but what the Holy Ghost [spirit] teaches, then we can compare spiritual things with spiritual because we have holy spirit in us. Then in verse 14 he says, "But the natural man receiveth not the things of the Spirit of God: for they are foolishness unto him: neither can he know them, because they [things of God] are spiritually discerned." It takes the holy spirit, the gift of Christ in us, to reveal spiritual things. A natural man, which we all were at the time of our birth, doesn't have the holy spirit within him and therefore the things of God are foolishness because he can't discern them. This does not mean that a natural man can't learn about the things of God otherwise no one could get born again. Romans 10:

> 13 For whosoever shall call upon the name of the Lord shall be saved.

> 14 How then shall they call on him in whom they have not believed? and how shall they believe in him of whom they have not heard? and how shall they hear without a preacher?

> 15 And how shall they preach, except they be sent? as it is written, How beautiful are the feet of them that preach the gospel of peace, and bring glad tidings of good things!

> 16 But they have not all obeyed the gospel. For Esaias saith, Lord, who hath believed our report?

> 17 So then faith cometh by hearing, and hearing by the word of God.

A natural man of body and soul can hear about Jesus by the preaching of the Word. He then makes a decision based upon what he hears and then can choose to make a choice. He can also choose to reject what he hears. We have seen in Romans the process of how to get born again. Romans 10:

9 That if thou shalt confess with thy mouth the Lord Jesus, and shalt believe in thine heart that God hath raised him from the dead, thou shalt be saved.

10 For with the heart man believeth unto righteousness; and with the mouth confession is made unto salvation.

At that moment a person becomes born again receiving the gift of holy spirit. I John 5:

1 Whosoever believeth that Jesus is the Christ is born of God: and every one that loveth him that begat loveth him also that is begotten of him.

1 John 3:

1 Behold, what manner of love the Father hath bestowed upon us, that we should be called the sons of God: therefore the world knoweth us not, because it knew him not.

2 Beloved, now are we the sons of God, and it doth not yet appear what we shall be: but we know that, when he shall appear, we shall be like him; for we shall see him as he is.

This being called sons of God, is for us *now!!!!!!*

Benefits That Come With Being Born Again

Just as there are benefits of being a son of a king or a wealthy father, there are benefits that come with being a child of God. It's one thing to maybe know what comes with the new birth but it is another to receive them and apply them in our lives. We have been so schooled to thing that we are unworthy in the eyes of God that we don't tap into what was given to us at the time of our new birth. It does us no good to have a million dollars in the bank if we don't use it. So let's look at some of the benefits of being a child of God. 1 Corinthians 1:

30 But of him are ye in Christ Jesus, who of God is made unto us wisdom, and righteousness, and sanctification, and redemption:

31 That, according as it is written, He that glorieth, let him glory in the Lord.

God has made this unto us. We didn't earn it. It is part of our sonship rights. First is wisdom. God's wisdom is available to us if we will ask for it. James 1:

5 If any of you lack wisdom, let him ask of God, that giveth to all men liberally, and upbraideth not; and it shall be given him.

Are you in a situation that you don't quite know how to handle? Ask of God and He will give you the wisdom to handle it. Next is righteousness. Righteousness is being in right standing. This is not just any righteousness. 2 Corinthians 5:

19 To wit, that God was in Christ, reconciling the world unto himself, not imputing their trespasses unto them; and hath committed unto us the word of reconciliation.

20 Now then we are ambassadors for Christ, as though God did beseech you by us: we pray you in Christ's stead, be ye reconciled to God.

21 For he hath made him to be sin for us, who knew no sin; that we might be made the righteousness of God in him.

God was at work in Jesus, to reconcile [bring back] the world to Himself. He doesn't hold our trespasses against us. He, in fact has given us *His* righteousness. And even if we do sin, miss the mark, He gives us a way back. I John 1:

> 7 But if we walk in the light, as he is in the light, we have fellowship one with another, and the blood of Jesus Christ his Son cleanseth us from all sin.

> 8 If we say that we have no sin, we deceive ourselves, and the truth is not in us.

> 9 If we confess our sins, he is faithful and just to forgive us our sins, and to cleanse us from all unrighteousness.

Being a human brings with it the ability to sin. For the believer it is broken fellowship with God. People can be squarely in direct opposition to the Word and yet think that they are ok. This person is deceived. But for us who realize that we have sinned, God has given us a way back. We simply confess our sins and God, through the work and blood of Jesus, cleanses us and puts us back in right standing with Him. If we sin, we don't lose the righteousness that we received, we simply are living outside of it and need to have our fellowship restored. Our sonship has two parts to it. Our standing and our state. Our standing with God is always that of a child, son of God. However, our state may fluctuate. We can be in fellowship with God, and then may mess up, breaking our fellowship but never our sonship. 1 John 1:

> 3 That which we have seen and heard declare we unto you, that ye also may have fellowship with us: and truly our fellowship is with the Father, and with his Son Jesus Christ.

4 And these things write we unto you, that your joy may be full.

God's heart for us is to have fellowship. Christianity is the way of a father with His children, not religious rules and regulations. The next thing made unto us is sanctification. This is God setting us apart from the world. Remember Colossians 1:

12 Giving thanks unto the Father, which hath made us meet [adequate] to be partakers of the inheritance of the saints in light:

13 Who hath delivered us from the power of darkness, and hath translated us into the kingdom of his dear Son:

God made us adequate by the work of His son and He delivered us from the power of darkness, and translated [transported if you will] us into the kingdom of his dear Son. This is while we still live here. But we must renew our minds and calm our sonship rights or the adversary will steal, kill and destroy them and keep us from using them.

The next thing that God has made unto us is redemption. Redemption is to have the price paid for. When I was a boy at certain stores when you checked out you would receive, depending on the amount of money spent, S&H Green Stamps. You would then paste these into a Green Stamp book which when full would be worth a certain amount. You would then go the S&H Green Stamp store and redeem them for merchandise. Maybe a toaster. You would pay for the toaster with your books of stamps, thus redeeming them. I can still remember going with my mother to the store. This is what Christ did for us. He paid the price, redeeming us.

Galatians 3:

> 13 Christ hath redeemed us from the curse of the law, being made a curse for us: for it is written, Cursed is every one that hangeth on a tree:

We are no longer under the curse. Why do so many Christians still live cursed lives? Lives with sickness, poverty, lack. Because they don't realize that they have a sonship right of redemption and claim it. Psalms 107:

> 2 Let the redeemed of the LORD say so, whom he hath redeemed from the hand of the enemy.

Psalms 136:

> 24 And hath redeemed us from our enemies: for his mercy endureth for ever.

Let us proclaim in the face of our enemy, our redemption because, He has delivered us from the hand of the enemy. Why? Because His mercy endures forever. Let's look at some of the other things that God has given unto us. 2 Peter 1:

> 3 According as his divine power hath given unto us all things that pertain unto life and godliness, through the knowledge of him that hath called us to glory and virtue.

God is not holding back anything from us. He wants us to live lives that glorify Him. However, it is dependent on how much of the Word we know and apply. Romans 12:

> 3 For I say, through the grace given unto me, to every man that is among you, not to think of himself more highly than he

ought to think; but to think soberly, according as God hath dealt to every man the measure of faith.

What measure of faith do we have? Galatians 2:

20 I am crucified with Christ: nevertheless I live; yet not I, but Christ liveth in me: and the life which I now live in the flesh I live by the faith of the Son of God, who loved me, and gave himself for me.

It's the faith of Jesus Christ. We have the potential to believe like Jesus did, but we must exercise it by renewing our minds. All that God did in Jesus is ours, if we will claim it as a son. Remember Ephesians 2:

8 For by grace are ye saved through faith; and that not of yourselves: it is the gift of God:

All that is given to us by God is by His divine favor. Also, part of our sonship rights include the manifestations of the spirit. 1 Corinthians 12:

7 But the manifestation of the Spirit is given to every man to profit withal.

8 For to one is given by the Spirit the word of wisdom; to another the word of knowledge by the same Spirit;

9 To another faith by the same Spirit; to another the gifts of healing by the same Spirit;

10 To another the working of miracles; to another prophecy; to another discerning of spirits; to another divers kinds of tongues; to another the interpretation of tongues:

11 But all these worketh that one and the selfsame Spirit, dividing to every man severally as he [the man or woman] will.

These manifestations are operations of the Christ in us, to give us victory over the adversary. However they are only in operation, *as we will.* It's up to us. With these sonship rights how can we approach God? Hebrews 4:

14 Seeing then that we have a great high priest, that is passed into the heavens, Jesus the Son of God, let us hold fast our profession [confession].

15 For we have not an high priest which cannot be touched with the feeling of our infirmities; but was in all points tempted like as we are, yet without sin.

16 Let us therefore come boldly unto the throne of grace, that we may obtain mercy, and find grace to help in time of need.

God doesn't want us to come to him beggarly. The adversary has done his best to convince Christians that they are unworthy of receiving God's grace and mercy. We have to rise up and take a stand, claiming our sonship rights to live in the favor that God has for us and destroy the works of the devil.

Being Born Again Of The Devil

While we have studied the subject of being born again of God, we need to look into the little know subject in God's Word, and that is the subject of being born again of the devil. Jesus was aware of this and dealt with it while here on earth. While it took until the day of Pentecost for people to be able to be born again of God's spirit, due to the work of Jesus Christ, the adversary has had the ability since the beginning. Remember what God said to the devil after the fall? Genesis 3:

> 14 And the LORD God said unto the serpent, Because thou hast done this, thou art cursed above all cattle, and above every beast of the field; upon thy belly shalt thou go, and dust shalt thou eat all the days of thy life:

> 15 And I will put enmity between thee and the woman, and between thy seed and her seed; it shall bruise thy head, and thou shalt bruise his heel.

How can a woman have seed? She can't, but look at Galatians 3:

> 16 Now to Abraham and his seed were the promises made. He saith not, And to seeds, as of many; but as of one, And to thy seed, which is Christ.

Seed is referring to children. It is used throughout the Bible in this sense. The seed of the woman is the seed of holy spirit which makes a person a child of God upon the new birth. But what about the devil? Jesus dealt with this in John 8:

> 38 I speak that which I have seen with my Father: and ye do that which ye have seen with your father.

> 39 They answered and said unto him, Abraham is our father. Jesus saith unto them, If ye were Abraham's children, ye would do the works of Abraham.

> 40 But now ye seek to kill me, a man that hath told you the truth, which I have heard of God: this did not Abraham.

41 Ye do the deeds of your father. Then said they to him, We be not born of fornication; we have one Father, even God.

42 Jesus said unto them, If God were your Father, ye would love me: for I proceeded forth and came from God; neither came I of myself, but he sent me.

43 Why do ye not understand my speech? even because ye cannot hear my word.

44 Ye are of your father the devil, and the lusts of your father ye will do. He was a murderer from the beginning, and abode not in the truth, because there is no truth in him. When he speaketh a lie, he speaketh of his own: for he is a liar, and the father of it.

Jesus was dealing with the Pharisees, religious leaders of the time. They claimed they were decedents of Abraham. But Jesus was dealing with them from a spiritual point of view. When they said, "we be not born of fornication", they were referencing the fact that Jesus was conceived before Mary and Joseph were married. They said, "we have one Father, even God." This is a characteristic of a person born of the seed of the devil. They believe they are right. But they are absolutely deceived. "Why do ye not understand my speech? Even because, ye cannot hear my word". This is another characteristic of that kind of person. They cannot hear or receive truth. Then Jesus comes right out and says it, "ye are of your father the devil". The word "of" used here in the Greek is "ek" and denotes origin. If you picture a circle with a dot in the middle of it and draw a line from the dot out past the circle, the dot is "ek" It is the point of origin. This is the same word used in I John 5:1, when it refers to us being born of God. God is the origin of our new birth.

Jesus tells them, the lusts of your father ye will do. "He was a murderer from the beginning, and abode not in the truth, because there is no truth in him. When he speaketh a lie, he speaketh of his own: for he is a liar, and the father of it." Just as a child may mimic the characteristic of their parent, "boy he sure takes after his father", someone might say of a child, hopefully in a complimentary way, the children of the devil do the same. When we "take after" *our* father we will manifest His characteristics of love, grace, mercy, kindness etc. When a child of the devil manifest his characteristics they are, murder, lying, deceit, fornication and a multitude of evil.

Because the devil has had the ability of getting people born again of his spirit since the

beginning, there are references of them in the Bible. John references to one in his epistle.

I John 3:

> 10 In this the children of [ek] God are manifest, and the children of [ek] the devil: whosoever doeth not righteousness is not of God, neither he that loveth not his brother.

> 11 For this is the message that ye heard from the beginning, that we should love one another.

> 12 Not as Cain, who was of [ek] that wicked one, and slew his brother. And wherefore slew he him? Because his own works were evil, and his brother's righteous.

Cain opened his mind through jealousy. Remember that Lucifer's fall was due partly because of jealousy. It was this jealousy in Cain, that the devil used to prompt Cain into committing murder. Cain was the first person to be born again of the devil. Another was Jezebel.

I Kings 21:

> 12 They proclaimed a fast, and set Naboth on high among the people.

> 13 And there came in two men, children of Belial, and sat before him: and the men of Belial witnessed against him, even against Naboth, in the presence of the people, saying, Naboth did blaspheme God and the king. Then they carried him forth out of the city, and stoned him with stones, that he died.

> 14 Then they sent to Jezebel, saying, Naboth is stoned, and is dead.

> 15 And it came to pass, when Jezebel heard that Naboth was stoned, and was dead, that Jezebel said to Ahab, Arise, take possession of the vineyard of Naboth the Jezreelite, which he refused to give thee for money: for Naboth is not alive, but dead.

> 16 And it came to pass, when Ahab heard that Naboth was dead, that Ahab rose up to go down to the vineyard of Naboth the Jezreelite, to take possession of it.

Jezebel did much evil against Israel and God's people. She wanted this vineyard that Naboth had but would not sell. So she set up false witnesses. Notice in verse 13 that it says, "and there came in two men, children of Belial". These are "seed boys" as I call them. Notice what they did. "The men of Belial witnessed against him". They lied.

DEAN J. SANDELL

The end result was that Naboth was murdered by stoning. Jezebel then told Ahab to go and take possession of the vineyard of Naboth. "And it came to pass, when Ahab heard that Naboth was dead, that Ahab rose up to go down to the vineyard of Naboth the Jezreelite, to take possession of it." Jezebel orchestrated the murder of Naboth so that she could steal the vineyard of Haboth. Seed boys will influence other people to do their bidding for them. Remember John 10:10. The thief comes not but for to steal, kill and destroy. 2 Kings 9:

> 22 And it came to pass, when Joram saw Jehu, that he said, Is it peace, Jehu? And he answered, What peace, so long as the whoredoms of thy mother Jezebel and her witchcrafts are so many?

Again we see the characteristics of a person born again of the adversary. Jezebels end was not so pleasant through. 2 Kings 9:

> 30 And when Jehu was come to Jezreel, Jezebel heard of it; and she painted her face, and tired her head, and looked out at a window.

> 31 And as Jehu entered in at the gate, she said, Had Zimri peace, who slew his master?

> 32 And he lifted up his face to the window, and said, Who is on my side? who? And there looked out to him two or three eunuchs.

> 33 And he said, Throw her down. So they threw her down: and some of her blood was sprinkled on the wall, and on the horses: and he trode her under foot.

34 And when he was come in, he did eat and drink, and said, Go, see now this cursed woman, and bury her: for she is a king's daughter.

35 And they went to bury her: but they found no more of her than the skull, and the feet, and the palms of her hands.

36 Wherefore they came again, and told him. And he said, This is the word of the LORD, which he spake by his servant Elijah the Tishbite, saying, In the portion of Jezreel shall dogs eat the flesh of Jezebel:

37 And the carcase of Jezebel shall be as dung upon the face of the field in the portion of Jezreel; so that they shall not say, This is Jezebel.

Notice in verse 34 that she is called a "cursed woman." God in the end will have vengeance upon the adversary. And he knows it!! Jezebel may be dead, but the spirit that worked in her is alive and working in our present time. They will meet their end at the final judgment along with all the people born again of his spirit.

So how does a person become born again of the seed of the adversary? The offer was made to Jesus in the wilderness during his temptations. Matthew 4:

8 Again, the devil taketh him up into an exceeding high mountain, and sheweth him all the kingdoms of the world, and the glory of them;

9 And saith unto him, All these things will I give thee, if thou wilt fall down and worship me.

10 Then saith Jesus unto him, Get thee hence, Satan: for it is written, Thou shalt worship the Lord thy God, and him only shalt thou serve.

This was no idle offer. It was genuine because as we have seen before that the adversary is the god of this world. The offer stills stands today to anyone who will accept it. When we are born into this world as a natural being, body and soul, we have three choices we can make. We can choose neither God or the devil and, will remain simply a natural man at our death. But we can also chose to worship God and accept His gift of salvation by confessing Jesus as lord and believing God raised Him from the dead. We then get born again of God's spirit, receiving eternal life. Or a person can confess Satan as lord and receive eternal damnation. Now no one in their right mind would confess the devil as lord. Yes I know there are Satan worshipers and they may or may not be born of the adversary, but most likely this birth takes place when they accept the offer of "the kingdoms of the world, and the glory of them." When a person sells out to the adversary by accepting power, money, prestige, and putting it first and foremost in their lives they make a sold out commitment to the devil and this plants the seed of the serpent in them. This is not like the holy spirit we receive which is an all and all infusing of the Christ in us. This is a opening of the mind of the individual that gives the adversary cart blanch over the person, and the adversary can use him for his purposes and promote his agenda's in the earth. I was taught that these people operate behind the scenes and are not necessarily out in the open. I believe this is true, but I also believe that many times they are right in front of us openly if you have the eyes to see them, which God will give us by His holy spirit. Remember God does not want us ignorant to the adversaries' devices. 2 Corinthians 2:

11 Lest Satan should get an advantage of us: for we are not ignorant of his devices.

Jesus said in Matthew 7:

13 Enter ye in at the strait gate: for wide is the gate, and broad is the way, that leadeth to destruction, and many there be which go in thereat:

14 Because strait is the gate, and narrow is the way, which leadeth unto life, and few there be that find it.

15 Beware of false prophets, which come to you in sheep's clothing, but inwardly they are ravening wolves.

16 Ye shall know them by their fruits. Do men gather grapes of thorns, or figs of thistles?

17 Even so every good tree bringeth forth good fruit; but a corrupt tree bringeth forth evil fruit.

18 A good tree cannot bring forth evil fruit, neither can a corrupt tree bring forth good fruit.

19 Every tree that bringeth not forth good fruit is hewn down, and cast into the fire.

20 Wherefore by their fruits ye shall know them.

Notice Jesus tells us in verse 15, Beware of false prophets, which come to you in sheep's clothing, but inwardly they are ravening wolves. Some of the fruits seed people produce are mentioned in Galatians 5:

19 Now the works of the flesh are manifest, which are these; Adultery, fornication, uncleanness, lasciviousness,

20 Idolatry, witchcraft, hatred, variance, emulations, wrath, strife, seditions, heresies,

21 Envyings, murders, drunkenness, revellings, and such like: of the which I tell you before, as I have also told you in time past, that they which do such things shall not inherit the kingdom of God.

Now don't go off half cocked and think that if someone commits adultery or murder, drunkenness, they are born again of the devil. Natural man and even Christians can do these things. I'm just pointing out who is behind this behavior. When you see someone who is promoting things that are in direct contraction to God's Word, beware. Open your eyes and if you want to know, God will show you. Don't forget that you have the manifestation of discerning of spirits, so that you won't be fooled. Remember it's the adversary who blinds the minds of people. Regarding fruit, we also as children of God can display fruit in our lives. Galatians 5:

22 But the fruit of the Spirit is love, joy, peace, longsuffering, gentleness, goodness, faith,

23 Meekness, temperance: against such there is no law.

24 And they that are Christ's have crucified the flesh with the affections and lusts.

25 If we live in the Spirit, let us also walk in the Spirit.

26 Let us not be desirous of vain glory, provoking one another, envying one another.

These are the fruits that we as sons of God can manifest in our lives. I mentioned that we can have the wisdom of God. Well there is another wisdom that is available also James 3:

14 But if ye have bitter envying and strife in your hearts, glory not, and lie not against the truth.

15 This wisdom descendeth not from above, but is earthly, sensual, devilish.

16 For where envying and strife is, there is confusion and every evil work.

17 But the wisdom that is from above is first pure, then peaceable, gentle, and easy to be intreated, full of mercy and good fruits, without partiality, and without hypocrisy.

18 And the fruit of righteousness is sown in peace of them that make peace.

You can see here the difference between the adversary's fruits and God's, and also the corresponding results. Envy, strife, confusion and, every evil work. Compared to, pure, then peaceable, gentle, and easy to be entreated, full of mercy and good fruits, without partiality, and without hypocrisy.

If we have enough Word in our minds and hearts, we will know just by the outward manifestation of what is going on around us to discern good and evil. Before I close this discussion I want to look at the ....

The Unforgiveable Sin

Mark 3:

28 Verily I say unto you, All sins shall be forgiven unto the sons of men, and blasphemies wherewith soever they shall blaspheme:

29 But he that shall blaspheme against the Holy Ghost hath never forgiveness, but is in danger of eternal damnation:

The Greek word for blaspheme is the word, blasphēmeō and means, to vilify; specially, to speak impiously, defame, rail on, revile, speak evil. When a person makes the devil lord in his life, he has committed the ultimate defaming of our father. Again this is not necessarily a outward reviling of God, but a total commitment to the devil, thus rejecting God and His mercy and grace. God's mercy and grace it able to forgive any sin. For the unsaved person their sins are forgiven upon the new birth, and subsequent sins are forgiven as a believer confesses them asking for forgiveness and are put back in right standing, fellowship, with their father God, and this is possible because of the seed of Christ in you. However, because a person born again of the devil has committed the ultimate sin against God, that sin and all subsequent sins committed cannot be forgiven because of the seed of the devil is in that person. The word "danger" in verse 29 is the Greek word, "enochos", and means, bound, under obligation, subject to, liable. Jesus referenced this when speaking to the Pharisees John 5:

28 Marvel not at this: for the hour is coming, in the which all that are in the graves shall hear his voice,

29 And shall come forth; they that have done good, unto the resurrection of life; and they that have done evil, unto the resurrection of damnation.

All people will stand before God. Our sins have been paid for by Jesus and we will be rewarded for our walk and go unto resurrection of life. Those born again of the adversary will go onto damnation. I John 5:

16 If any man see his brother sin a sin which is not unto death, he shall ask, and he shall give him life for them that sin not unto death. There is a sin unto death: I do not say that he shall pray for it.

It is of no use to pray for a person who is born again of the adversary. Just as we are sealed by the Christ in us unto everlasting life, the person born of the devil is sealed unto eternal damnation. If you see a brother or sister in Christ not living up to their potential, or a person who is not yet born again of God, you can pray for them.

We have learned in this study about being born again of God's Spirit and the benefits of that new birth. We also learned about being born again of the devil and the consequences of that birth. I feel it is important to understand both so that we can walk in victory in our lives. As I close this chapter, I want to end by pointing out another one of our sonship rights. II Corinthians 5:

17 Therefore if any man be in Christ, he is a new creature: old things are passed away; behold, all things are become new.

18 And all things are of God, who hath reconciled us to himself by Jesus Christ, and hath given to us the ministry of reconciliation.

DEAN J. SANDELL

Since God reconciled us to Himself by Jesus Christ, it is our privilege to reconcile others to Christ. We can bring people to salvation by preaching the good news of the gospel. God has not only given us this ministry but the tools to carry it out. II Corinthians 5:

> 19 To wit, that God was in Christ, reconciling the world unto himself, not imputing their trespasses unto them; and hath committed unto us the word of reconciliation.

God has committed unto us the "word of reconciliation". The only thing that will reconcile a person back to God is, God's Word which we can speak forth to others so that they may enjoy the sonship and fellowship that God wants for them. I Timothy 2:

> 4 Who will have all men to be saved, and to come unto the knowledge of the truth.

> 5 For there is one God, and one mediator between God and men, the man Christ Jesus.

Christ is the mediator, we are the ones who can enlighten people with an accurate knowledge of the Word. Let's claim our rightful sonship rights and then proclaim them to others so that they too can enjoy them.

CHAPTER 13

The Two Kingdoms

Ephesians 6:

> 10 Finally, my brethren, be strong in the Lord, and in the power of his might.

> 11 Put on the whole armour of God, that ye may be able to stand against the wiles of the devil.

> 12 For we wrestle not against flesh and blood, but against principalities, against powers, against the rulers of the darkness of this world, against spiritual wickedness in high places.

1 Peter 5:

> 8 Be sober, be vigilant; because your adversary the devil, as a roaring lion, walketh about, seeking whom he may devour:

WE HAVE STUDIED a lot and learned a lot about the adversary, but I feel it very important to understand the battle that is being raged around us, and at us, and our weapons that we can use.

I want to point out that there are really four kingdoms. There is the plant kingdom, the animal kingdom, the kingdom of man and the spiritual kingdom. Each supersedes the other. The animal kingdom and the kingdom of man rule over the plant kingdom. Man rules over the animal kingdom (as a general rule), and the spiritual kingdom is superior to the other three kingdoms. In the spiritual kingdom there are two kingdoms. The kingdom of God, and the kingdom of darkness. The kingdom of God rules over the kingdom of darkness *when* we operate according to the kingdom of God rules. If we are not aware of the way that God's kingdom works, then we will be ruled by the kingdom of darkness. Acts 26:

> 18 To open their eyes, and to turn them from darkness to light, and from the power of Satan unto God, that they may receive forgiveness of sins, and inheritance among them which are sanctified by faith that is in me.

God wants our eyes open to know what is going on and to deliver us from the power of Satan unto God so that God can work in our lives.

We need to know something very vital about God. 1 John 1:

> 5 This then is the message which we have heard of him, and declare unto you, that God is light, and in him is no darkness at all.

We cannot forget that God is light. There is no darkness in Him. All darkness whether it be small or great is from the adversary. If we don't understand this then we will be confused and subject to the adversaries tricks. James 1:

> 17 Every good gift and every perfect gift is from above, and cometh down from the Father of lights, with whom is no variableness, neither shadow of turning.

It's every good gift and every perfect gift that comes from God who is the father of lights. Also, God is not wishy washy. He is stable and can be counted upon because there is not shadow of turning. He is always trust worthy. The adversary is the one who will adapt himself to fit the situation that he is trying to control. If it fits to be crafty, then he will be crafty. If it fits to lie then he will lie. He will change to fit the circumstances. This is why he *can't* be trusted. But look what God wants for us. Ephesians 1:

> 18 The eyes of your understanding being enlightened; that ye may know what is the hope of his calling, and what the riches of the glory of his inheritance in the saints.

Gods will is so that our eyes, spiritual eyes, are enlightened. Giving us light.

II Corinthians 4:

> 6 For God, who commanded the light to shine out of darkness, hath shined in our hearts, to give the light of the knowledge of the glory of God in the face of Jesus Christ.

God is not the one who is keeping us in darkness. Our light comes from a knowledge, accurate knowledge, of Him and Jesus Christ. John 8:

> 12 Then spake Jesus again unto them, saying, I am the light of the world: he that followeth me shall not walk in darkness, but shall have the light of life.

Jesus is the light of the world because he walked in the light of God's Word. He also did something for us. Colossians 1:

13 Who hath delivered us from the power of darkness, and hath translated us into the kingdom of his dear Son.

It was by his work that we can be delivered from the power of darkness. God also informs us that we are in a warfare, battle, while we are living here. 2 Corinthians 10:

3 For though we walk in the flesh, we do not war after the flesh:

4 (For the weapons of our warfare are not carnal, but mighty through God to the pulling down of strong holds;) [mind sets that are contray to the word

5 Casting down imaginations, and every high thing that exalteth itself against the knowledge of God, and bringing into captivity every thought to the obedience of Christ.

Paul instructed Timothy regarding this warfare. I Timothy 1:

18 This charge I commit unto thee, son Timothy, according to the prophecies which went before on thee, that thou by them mightest war a good warfare;

As we see what is going on in this present world, we need to look behind the scenes and see what is going on in the spiritual world. We are equipped by God to do this. He tells us in Corinthians that our weapons in the warfare are not carnal, of the flesh, because we are not dealing with flesh and blood but with forces of darkness in the spirit realm. It may look like it is people, which it is because the adversary needs people to carry out his mission, but when we are spiritually minded we will see what is behind it and then we can stand against them. How? *Casting down imaginations, and every high thing that exalteth itself against the knowledge of God, and bringing into captivity every thought to the obedience of Christ.* We take captive our imagination which is made up of words. When our imagination puts itself above the Word we need to bring it in check and take it captive by putting the Word on. Romans 8:

31 What shall we then say to these things? If God *be* for us, who *can be* against us?

32 He that spared not his own Son, but delivered him up for us all, how shall he not with him also freely give us all things?

33 Who shall lay any thing to the charge of God's elect? *It is* God that justifieth.

34 Who is he that condemneth? *It is* Christ that died, yea rather, that is risen again, who is even at the right hand of God, who also maketh intercession for us.

35 Who shall separate us from the love of Christ? shall tribulation, or distress, or persecution, or famine, or nakedness, or peril, or sword?

36 As it is written, For thy sake we are killed all the day long; we are accounted as sheep for the slaughter.

37 Nay, in all these things we are more than conquerors through him that loved us.

38 For I am persuaded, that neither death, nor life, nor angels, nor principalities, nor powers, nor things present, nor things to come,

39 Nor height, nor depth, nor any other creature, shall be able to separate us from the love of God, which is in Christ Jesus our Lord.

That is quite a list of things that can come against us. Whatever it may be that is coming against you can be overcome because, in verse 37 God says emphatically *NAY!!!!!!* In all things we are more than conquerors. Verse 38 Paul writes, *for I am persuaded.* Are we persuaded, convinced beyond a shadow of a doubt, or are we mentally ascending to it?

I John 3:

8 He that committeth sin is of the devil; for the devil sinneth from the beginning. For this purpose the Son of God was manifested,

Do you see here the purpose for Jesus coming to earth? *That he might destroy the works of the devil.* But He needs us to cooperate. It is up to us to stand against the wiles of the devil. God has given us the means and weapons to do this. Among these and of primary importance are the manifestations of the spirit that we received when we got born again. I Corinthians 12:

7 But the manifestation of the Spirit is given to every man to profit withal.

8 For to one is given by the Spirit the word of wisdom; to another the word of knowledge by the same Spirit;

9 To another faith by the same Spirit; to another the gifts of healing by the same Spirit;

10 To another the working of miracles; to another prophecy; to another discerning of spirits; to another divers kinds of tongues; to another the interpretation of tongues:

11 But all these worketh that one and the selfsame Spirit, dividing to every man severally as he [the man/woman]will.

It is through the usage of the manifestations that we get the advantage over our adversary. One of those manifestations is discerning of spirits. God can and will reveal to us the presence of spirits. Then by the manifestations of word of knowledge and word of wisdom, He will show us how to handle a situation. Just a note about those manifestations of word of wisdom and word of knowledge. They are also there to help us in our everyday lives to help us to walk. Another weapon in our warfare is faith. I John 4:

4 Ye are of God, little children, and have overcome them: because greater is he that is in you, than he that is in the world.

1 John 5:

4 For whatsoever is born of God overcometh the world: and this is the victory that overcometh the world, even our faith.

God is very aware of the presence of the adversary, but He informs us that we have overcome them [the adversary] because of the Christ in us. He then tells us what we have to overcome the world and that is our faith, believing. Believing what? God's Word over the adversaries' words. We also have to recognize that we have been given authority on this earth to exercise our rights as sons of God. 1 John 3:

DEAN J. SANDELL

1 Behold, what manner of love the Father hath bestowed upon us, that we should be called the sons of God: therefore the world knoweth us not, because it knew him not.

2 Beloved, now are we the sons of God, and it doth not yet appear what we shall be: but we know that, when he shall appear, we shall be like him; for we shall see him as he is.

3 And every man that hath this hope in him purifieth himself, even as he is pure.

When are we the sons of God? NOW!!! In the future we will be like Jesus in our glorified bodies, but now while we are still living here we are truly sons of God. We need to operate in that authority. Luke 10:

17 And the seventy returned again with joy, saying, Lord, even the devils are subject unto us through thy name.

18 And he said unto them, I beheld Satan as lightning fall from heaven.

19 Behold, I give unto you power to tread on serpents and scorpions, and over all the power of the enemy: and nothing shall by any means hurt you.

20 Notwithstanding in this rejoice not, that the spirits are subject unto you; but rather rejoice, because your names are written in heaven.

Jesus had sent out disciples and they were filled with joy because they discovered that devils were subject to them. And remember that they weren't even born again. He says in verse 19, *I give unto you power to tread on serpents and scorpions, and over all the power of the enemy: and nothing shall by any means hurt you.* If they had that kind of power in that administration, what do you think we have as born again sons of God? Luke 9:

> 1 Then he called his twelve disciples together, and gave them power and authority over all devils, and to cure diseases.

> 2 And he sent them to preach the kingdom of God, and to heal the sick.

What about us. Everything that is not of God is of the devil. Diseases, poverty, lack, depression. Anything that is at odds with God's Word we have authority over it. Remember this was all in God's original design. Genesis 1:

> 26 And God said, Let us make man in our image, after our likeness: and let them have dominion over the fish of the sea, and over the fowl of the air, and over the cattle, and over all the earth, and over every creeping thing that creepeth upon the earth.

> 27 So God created man in his own image, in the image of God created he him; male and female created he them.

> 28 And God blessed them, and God said unto them, Be fruitful, and multiply, and replenish the earth, and subdue it: and have dominion over the fish of the sea, and over the fowl of the air, and over every living thing that moveth upon the earth.

It is up to use to exercise this dominion. Jesus did the work for us. Now we have to put this on in our minds. As we put the Word on in our minds, we have to make a decision as we have looked at before, to walk in it. Galatians 5:

DEAN J. SANDELL

16 This I say then, Walk in the Spirit, and ye shall not fulfill the lust of the flesh.

It's through our five senses that the adversary attacks us, so if we learn to walk by the spirit we will be able to defeat him.

Another weapon in our arsenal is the name of Jesus. When we got born again, we received the power of attorney to use the name of Jesus. Let's look again at Luke 10:

17 And the seventy returned again with joy, saying, Lord, even the devils are subject unto us through thy name.

This was during the Christ administration, and the devils were subject to the seventy using Jesus' name. What about our administration of Grace? The legal definition of Power of Attorney is, "the authority to act for another person in specified or all legal or financial matters."

The Power of Attorney that we have been given is, to legally use the name of Jesus in dealing with spiritual matters here on earth while we await the return of Jesus. The power is limited only to the extent of the resources behind the name. Philippians 2:

9 Wherefore God also hath highly exalted him, and given him a name which is above every name:

10 That at the name of Jesus every knee should bow, of things in heaven, and things in earth, and things under the earth;

When God says, "every knee should bow" that's just what He means. That means the "name" of every disease, physically, mentally, and spiritually. The "names", lack, poverty must bow. What are the resources that are behind the name. Ephesians 1:

19 And what is the exceeding greatness of his power to us-ward who believe, according to the working of his mighty power,

20 Which he wrought in Christ, when he raised him from the dead, and set him at his own right hand in the heavenly places,

21 Far above all principality, and power, and might, and dominion, and every name that is named, not only in this world, but also in that which is to come:

22 And hath put all things under his feet, and gave him to be the head over all things to the church,

23 Which is his body, the fulness of him that filleth all in all.

He/we are "seated with him at his [God's] own right hand in the heavenly places." He/we are, "far above all principality, and power, and might, and dominion, and every name that is named, not only in this world, but also in that which is to come." He/we have "all things under his [our] feet, and gave him [Jesus] to be the head over all things to the church."

Let's see what Jesus told his disciples. John 14:

12 Verily, verily, I say unto you, He that believeth on me, the works that I do shall he do also; and greater works than these shall he do; because I go unto my Father.

13 And whatsoever ye shall ask in my name, that will I do, that the Father may be glorified in the Son.

14 If ye shall ask any thing in my name, I will do it.

Jesus here, is instruction his disciples to use his name when asking anything of the Father, according to the Word, so that God may be glorified. God wants us to us Jesus' name. Look at what else Jesus told his disciples. Luke 10:

> 19 Behold, I give unto you power [authority] to tread on serpents and scorpions, and over all the power of the enemy: and nothing shall by any means hurt you.

Because of what Jesus did, we have authority over the enemy. But we must use it. In war, a solider is given a gun to fight the enemy. He is also given the "authority" to use it in battle to kill the enemy. If he doesn't exercise his authority, and kill the enemy the enemy will kill him. We can't kill our enemy. God will take care of that in the future. But we can destroy his works in our lives by using our God given authority over him by using the name of Jesus in our dealing with him. 1 John 3:

> 8 He that committeth sin is of the devil; for the devil sinneth from the beginning. For this purpose the Son of God was manifested, that he might destroy the works of the devil.

We not only have the authority, *BUT*, we also have the power. Speak the name of Jesus against any name that the adversary brings against you and expect it to be taken care of. Don't be shy about this. If God says that we can come "boldly" unto his throne of grace, how do you think we are to come up against the adversaries' kingdom?

Pray in Jesus name to the Father, and use the name of Jesus in the devils face to put him where he belongs. Which is under your heal. Don't be concerned about offending God when you use Jesus' name, you won't. But you certainly will offend the adversary.

One other weapon and probably the most powerful is found in Ephesians 5:

> 2 And walk in love, as Christ also hath loved us, and hath given himself for us an offering and a sacrifice to God for a sweetsmelling savour.

1 Corinthians 13:

> 13 And now abideth faith, hope, charity, these three; but the greatest of these is charity.

1 John 4:

> 18 There is no fear in love; but perfect love casteth out fear:

This is our greatest weapon because love overcomes evil. This love, is the word in the Greek, agapa. It means by usage, the love of God in the renewed mind in manifestation. It is us deciding to love the way God loves. 1 Corinthians 13:

> 1 Though I speak with the tongues of men and of angels, and have not charity, I am become as sounding brass, or a tinkling cymbal.

> 2 And though I have the gift of prophecy, and understand all mysteries, and all knowledge; and though I have all faith, so that I could remove mountains, and have not charity, I am nothing.

> 3 And though I bestow all my goods to feed the poor, and though I give my body to be burned, and have not charity, it profiteth me nothing.

DEAN J. SANDELL

4 Charity suffereth long, and is kind; charity envieth not; charity vaunteth not itself, is not puffed up,

5 Doth not behave itself unseemly, seeketh not her own, is not easily provoked, thinketh no evil;

6 Rejoiceth not in iniquity, but rejoiceth in the truth;

7 Beareth all things, believeth all things, hopeth all things, endureth all things.

8 Charity never faileth: but whether there be prophecies, they shall fail; whether there be tongues, they shall cease; whether there be knowledge, it shall vanish away.

9 For we know in part, and we prophesy in part.

10 But when that which is perfect is come, then that which is in part shall be done away.

As we walk in love we will be victorious in our lives. God has given us all we need to defeat the enemy. It's up to us to use these tools to receive all that God has for us and to reject what the adversary desires for us.

CHAPTER 14

Having Done All Stand

WE HAVE LEARNED a lot in our study of the Word of God. We learned how we received the Word, that the Word can be trusted. We have learned a lot about God himself. We know that God is good and that God is love. We have learned God wants the best for us. In closing I want to leave you with a couple of prayers that Paul wrote under the guidance of God. Ephesians 1:

> 15 Wherefore I also, after I heard of your faith in the Lord Jesus, and love unto all the saints,

> 16 Cease not to give thanks for you, making mention of you in my prayers;

> 17 That the God of our Lord Jesus Christ, the Father of glory, may give unto you the spirit of wisdom and revelation in the knowledge of him:

As we acquire more knowledge of God, through an accurate study of the Word, God will be able to give us the spirit of wisdom, how to act wisely, and revelation, God giving us information regarding Him or a situation.

> 18 The eyes of your understanding being enlightened; that ye may know what is the hope of his calling, and what the riches of the glory of his inheritance in the saints,

DEAN J. SANDELL

19 And what is the exceeding greatness of his power to us-ward
   who believe, according to the working of his mighty power,

God wants us to know. He wants our eyes enlightened not darkened
by the adversary. He wants us to *know*, not guess about the hope of
his calling. To *know* the riches of the glory of His inheritance in the
saints. We as believers are important to God. He wants us to *know*
the exceeding greatness of His power toward us and the working of
His mighty power in our lives.

20 Which he wrought in Christ, when he raised him from the
   dead, and set him at his own right hand in the heavenly places,

21 Far above all principality, and power, and might, and
   dominion, and every name that is named, not only in this
   world, but also in that which is to come:

22 And hath put all things under his feet, and gave him to be
   the head over all things to the church,

23 Which is his body, the fulness of him that filleth all in all.

God did this for us through Christ. When He raised Jesus from the
dead we were raised with him. When He set Jesus at His own right
hand in heavenly places we were set also. When He placed Jesus far
above all principality, and power, and might, and dominion, and
every name that is named, not only in this world, but also in that
which is to come, we were also. When He had put all things under
his feet, they were put under our feet. We have so much power over
the adversary, if we will only use it. Ephesians 3:

14 For this cause I bow my knees unto the Father of our Lord
   Jesus Christ,

15 Of whom the whole family in heaven and earth is named,

16 That he would grant you, according to the riches of his glory, to be strengthened with might by his Spirit in the inner man;

This is God's will for us. To be strengthened with might, not be weak and beggarly. As we develop the inner man by walking by the spirit and renewing our minds, the inner man, Christ in us, will strengthen us. And this is done by our works? NO! By the riches of His glory.

17 That Christ may dwell in your hearts by faith; that ye, being rooted and grounded in love,

18 May be able to comprehend with all saints what is the breadth, and length, and depth, and height;

19 And to know the love of Christ, which passeth knowledge, that ye might be filled with all the fulness of God.

God wants us rooted and grounded. Not tossed about by every wind of doctrine of men who lie in wait to deceive us. He wants us to comprehend, again to know, every dimension of His and Christ's love for us which is so great that it passes knowledge. And He wants us filled with all the fullness of God. Can it be any clearer that God is on our side?

20 Now unto him that is able to do exceeding abundantly above all that we ask or think, according to the power that worketh in us,

21 Unto him be glory in the church by Christ Jesus throughout all ages, world without end. Amen.

How big can you ask and think? God is willing to do *exceeding abundantly* above it. And it is according to the power that works in

DEAN J. SANDELL

who? US! We have to activate that power by believing what God tells us in His Word of who we are and what we have. But it is up to us.

When we do this then God gets the justly deserved glory. And we do these things by Christ Jesus.

And in closing Ephesians 6:

> 10 Finally, my brethren, be strong in the Lord, and in the power of his might.

God is not asking us to be strong in and of ourselves, but in the Lord and the power of HIS might. God will back us up.

> 11 Put on the whole armour of God, that ye may be able to stand against the wiles of the devil.

We are not to put on just some of the armor but all of it so that we are fully equipped with the armor God has given us. Why? So that we can stand against the wiles of the devil. Remember that the secret of the devils success lies in the secrecy of his moves. God will give us what we need to know so that we will not be deceived.

> 12 For we wrestle not against flesh and blood, but against principalities, against powers, against the rulers of the darkness of this world, against spiritual wickedness [wicked spirits] in high places.

We have already looked at this but it bears repeating. We are not dealing with that wicked neighbor or that person at work that is giving us trouble. It is spiritual wickedness in high places. It's the rulers of the darkness in this world. But we can shine as lights because of the light of Christ in us.

13 Wherefore take unto you the whole armour of God, that ye may be able to withstand in the evil day, and having done all, to stand.

God is reminding us again to take on whole armor so that we can withstand in this evil day. And then we are told to stand. Not back down because God is standing with us.

14 Stand therefore, having your loins girt about with truth, and having on the breastplate of righteousness;

15 And your feet shod [covered] with the preparation of the gospel of peace;

We stand by having our loins, which is a figure of speech, representing the center of strength in the human body, "girt", or strengthen, if you will with truth. A "girt", in construction, is a lateral (horizontal) support put in a wall to give it strength, primarily, to resist wind loads.

When the storms of life come against us, that the adversary will try, that is when we "girt" up our minds. We strengthen ourselves by putting on the truth in our minds. The breastplate protects our heart, and we do that by putting on mentally our righteousness that we received when we got born again. And our feet are covered with the gospel, good news of peace, which we can bring to others so that they too can live an abundant life. Ephesians 6:

16 Above all, taking the shield of faith, wherewith ye shall be able to quench all the fiery darts of the wicked.

17 And take the helmet of salvation, and the sword of the Spirit, which is the word of God:

The thing that God wants us to take above all is the shield of faith. Remember that is faith that allows us to overcome the world. With the shield of faith we will be able to quench, put out, some, NOOOOO!!!!! All the fiery darts of the wicked. Fiery darts are the words that the adversary throws at us through people, the media, friends, neighbors, the person at work. If they are saying things contrary to God's Word, we use our shield of faith based upon the Word that we know and quench them. We then take the helmet of salvation, that wholeness that we received upon the new birth. And finally we take the sword of the Spirit, the Word of God. We wield it with our mouths. We speak, and yes out loud if the situation calls for it, the Word. At the very least we have to resist the fiery darts in our minds because that is the place of attacks. The definition of wield is: To handle (a weapon or tool,) with skill and ease; to exercise (authority or influence, effectively.) This is how we are to become with the Word. Skillful masters of the Word exercising our authority and influence over the adversary.

My final words of encouragement to you are: Ephesians 6:

> 13 Wherefore take unto you the whole armour of God, that ye may be able to withstand in the evil day, and having done all, ***TO STAND!!!!!!!!!!***

Thank you for taking the time to read this book. It is my heart's desire that it has informed you and given you an understanding of God and His Son Jesus Christ and God's Word. My hope is that it has given you the tools to fellowship with God and His son and to be victorious over the adversary in every category of your life.

God Bless You

Dean Sandell

Printed in the United States
By Bookmasters